Signs of the Tines

The Ultimate Astrological Cookbook

JOAN PORTE

Soulsign Publishing. LLC   ©2013   Burke, Virginia

Soulsign Publishing
Post Office Box 10517
Burke, Virginia, USA 20009

Printed in the United States, United Kingdom and Australia.
Distributed by Soulsign Publishing and Ingram Book Company.
ISBN-10: 0-9788535-1-2
ISBN-13: 978-0-9788535-1-8
Categorization:
1. Cooking: Regional & Ethnic – General   2. Body, Mind, Spirit: Astrology – General   3. Cooking: General

Cover design, interior design and layout by Tamian Wood, Beyond Design International, www.BeyondDesignInternational.com

acknowledgments

Non-Stock Photography by Eric G Brown
http://www.ericgbrown.com
Food Styling by Karl Schwartz
http://www.lagniappepcs.com
Editing by Rebecca Mashaw

I would like to extend special thanks to Karen Rugg of Karlynne Creative who was instrumental in coming up with the title of this book, edits and so many other things. http://www.karlynne.com

Thanks to my friends Kate Trygstad, Mimi Malfitano, Martha Trunk, Daphne Miller and Eva DeCourcey, for their appetites, willingness to comment on my food and unending encouragement. Also to my sister Jean Porte who helped me remember many of the old-time recipes. I couldn't have done it without all of you. My other friends who donated family recipes are mentioned throughout the book. Thank you all very much!

Contents

introduction

This book will be useful to anyone regardless of their astrological interest or culinary acuity. These recipes are taken from a number of sources; some are family gems handed down by my Italian-American mother, Jean Garofalo Porte; my grandmother, Philomena Rizzo Garofalo, and my Aunt Mary Garofalo De Flora. Others are from the treasure chests of friends and the rest I have concocted and tweaked over the years. With a few exceptions (darn those adventurous Sagittarians) they are uncomplicated and all are packed with taste.

I have been cooking since I was tall enough to reach my mother's counter and I watched her cook even before that. From the time I was about age three, she used to sit me on the counter as she worked. My mother's family were "by touch and sight" cooks. We would ask her how much salt to put in, for instance, and the response was, "Until it looks like there is enough." The question, "How much oil (or whatever) does this need?" was answered with, "Feel it and see." Getting a recipe from Mom was a real treat. You had to follow her around and stop her before she tossed something in the pot and make her measure it as she glared at you.

When I was thirteen my parents started to spend the winters in Florida. I couldn't wait to come home from school and prepare dinner for my older siblings. (Yes, I have heard every nerd joke that goes with that activity,

thank you very much!) So while I am not a classically trained cook by any means, I feel I have been in a very hands-on cooking school all my life.

I am a trained astrologer and have been studying the stars for more than 30 years. I have had the great good fortune to study under one of the most innovative and inspiring teachers in the business, Adam Gainsburg, founder of Soulsign Astrology®, http://www.soulsignastrology.com

By matching these two passions I hope to bring a new, fun twist to cooking and to give you some new ideas on entertaining. The more you know about your astrological chart or that of the person for whom you are cooking, the more fun you will have with this book. Everyone knows their Sun Sign – even those who will deny it – but a person's culinary appetites are more defined by their Rising Sign (also known as the Ascendant) and even further by their South Node. In fact, in the West, Sun Signs have been elevated to an importance they frankly don't deserve.

However, if all you know or care to know about Astrology is your Sun Sign, that is great – you will still find terrific cooking ideas here.

If, on the other hand, you find yourself confused when your Gemini spouse seems to gravitate more toward the

Virgo section of this cookbook, you may want take a further step into astrological gastronomy. For, without a full food analysis, you might not know that your Gemini really has Virgo rising and is more interested in the healthy Virgo food than the quick "on the run morsels" of the Gemini.

The Rising Sign is on the cusp – or mouth – of the 1st house, or the eastern-most side of your chart, hence the name "rising." The Sun "rises" in the east. More than any other placement on the chart, the Rising Sign shows how we project ourselves to the world. It is really the sign of personality.

Beyond just fun you can also use this cookbook to eat for health. What sign is on the cusp of your 6th house – the house of health? If it is Pisces, you are probably dealing with allergies, autoimmune diseases and illnesses that are hard to define and hard to diagnose. These ailments may even be from the subconscious. Capricorn will point more to depressive issues, Aries more to fevers. I have included a healthy recipe for each sign to give your system a boost.

You can even look at a person's 4th house to see how they use their homes to entertain. The 4th is the house of home life and our roots. My 4th house is ruled by Capricorn, so I use my home for lots of gatherings. I stuff my friends with food and send them home with doggie bags the size of Colorado. Why? Because Capricorn is the traditional sign of the provider, the archetypal father who must see that the family is fed and cared for in all of their material needs.

One of the fun things you can do with this book is have an Astrological Dinner Party (see page 9). Sit down and compare food and food charts. (For more on getting a full food chart analysis, see page 8.) You might find that the quirky Aquarian is craving the comfort food dictated by their Cancer South Node or that the secretive Scorpio is heeding their Rising Sign and happily scarfing down the hot and spicy Aries food.

I mentioned the South Node before, right? The North and South Nodes are odd little creatures. They are actually the invisible points on the lunar orbit that mark where the Moon intersects with the path of the Sun, or ecliptic. These quirky little characters actually tell us a lot in Karmic Astrology because they are windows into the past lives we have led (South Node) and the places our souls want to go in this life (North Node.) Chapter two has more information on the Nodes. However, as I said you don't have to take Astrology to its fullest or do the past life thing to have fun with this book. Add as little or as much as you would like, sort of like salt and pepper.

Part of the fun is to improvise. I would love to write a cookbook that says, "Here are the ingredients, now go play with them and make a great dish." Recipes are guidelines at best. If you are like me and don't like cilantro, try parsley. If you don't like green peppers, try red or leave them out. Play with your food! Recipes, unlike birth charts, are not written in the sky!

Whatever sign drives you the most – whether it is the Sun, Rising or South Node – grab the book, head to the kitchen and have fun! I have grouped the recipes by sign because that is the easiest way to look at them and it doesn't matter if you want to use Sun, Rising or any other house cusp, go to that section to find what you want. For instance, you can use the Aries section for Aries Sun, Rising, 4th house cusp or South Node, etc.

get your astrological chart
and your astrological food analysis

To order an astrological food analysis chart for you or a loved one visit http://www.signsofthetines.com.

I will need the time, place and date of birth for each person getting a foodie chart. If you don't have the time, try to get as close as you can. If you really don't know – we can do something called "rectification of the chart." Email me at astrologycook@signsofthetines.com for details.

I will email you a complete personal audio food chart analysis that is between 35 – 60 minutes long and can be downloaded and saved to an MP3 player, as well as a chart that you can print. Your chart will look something like the

one below with the planets and asteroids in the right place for you, of course.

If you are technologically phobic – oh how Pisces of you – or prefer to send a check, email me at astrologycook@signsofthetines.com and I will explain both how to order and other ways I can get the information to you.

Don't worry that this chart looks like ancient Norse. My audio analysis is in "real English" and I include a copy of my "Astro Notes" that identifies all of the symbols and describes the meaning of the houses.

FOODIE CHART
Event Chart
Oct 26 1955
6:25 am EDT +4:00
Paterson, New Jersey
40°N55' 074°W10'20"
Geocentric
Tropical
Placidus
Mean Node
Rating: AA

Compliments of
Joan's Astrology
astrologycook@signsofthetines.com
www.signsofthetines.com

8

host an astrological dinner party

Are you tired of the same old dinner party idea? Have you run out of ideas on how to have a fun foodie night? Then try an astrological dinner party night!

With my Astro Dinner Party Kit you will get:

- audio foodie chart interpretations (see page 8) for all of your guests,

- menus and recipes that are not contained in this book,

- decorating tips to make the party fun for the various signs at your table.

You will have the topic of conversation – your charts, menus and recipes. All you need to supply is the food and drink!

To order an Astro Dinner Party kit go to http://www.signsofthetines.com.

Remember that I will need the birth time, place and date for all attendees.

For parties with more than six people email me at astrologycook@signsofthetines.com

the sun
is only the beginning!

Chapter 1

You can be very Aquarian and take this book as far out in the universe as you want or stay as close to home with it as you feel comfortable, as any good Cancer would. If you want to stay with just Sun Sign cooking, skip the next few chapters that reveal more about Astrology and have at it. However, if you want to really delve further into cooking with the stars read on and then fire up the oven.

Somewhere between "Hey Daddy-O" of the '50s and "Can you dig it?" of the '70s, another obnoxious phrase came into the American lexicon; "Hey honey, what is your (Sun) Sign?" Sun Signs became all the rage for the pseudo-astrologically attuned. It was all about the Sun to the exclusion of the hundreds of other stars and asteroids whirling around the sky. There was a belief that if you knew what day a person was born you would know everything about them even down to the deepest secrets they were squirreling away in their psyche.

Don't get me wrong, there is nothing wrong with Sun Signs *per se*; they are useful little creatures to have when walking around the Zodiac. Sun Sign energy in an astrological chart adds flavor and an understanding of person's inner motivation. However, while the Sun is the center of our solar system, it is not the center of the Zodiac. It may be unfair and incongruous but that is just the way it works.

Think about that. There are twelve Sun Signs. How many people have been born since the first human stood upright – a couple of zillion billion, perhaps? So divide twelve into a couple of zillion billion. How can every single person who falls under each sign be exactly alike? Every Capricorn born since the beginning of mankind is not just like every other Capricorn who ever lived. All Librans who have ever existed are not cookie cutters of one another. Sun Sign Astrology alone is quite limited.

Those people pathologically attached to the Sun Sign as their only method of interpretation have done more than even the nay-sayers to screw up a fascinating, spiritual and deeply mystical art form. Because Sun Sign interpretation is so broad, it can't fit for a huge percentage of people. It is like saying all people with brown hair are football fans. This makes it very easy for people to become discouraged with the entire process and for the anti-Astrology crowd to do the "I told you so" routine.

When our astrological forefathers designed the astrological chart about seven or eight thousand years ago, they didn't sidle up to a young babe in a bar and say, "Hey honey, what is your Sun Sign?" That would have been unheard of! Instead they slid off their dromedaries and used the old pick-up line, "Hey baby, what is your Rising Sign?" The ancients did not pay a lot of attention to Sun energy. In fact the Sun got on their nerves a bit because it impeded their work. How can you look up into the sky and study the stars and planets with the big old Sun blaring into your eyes? The savvy ancients did their work at night when the Sun was "down" – so they didn't place a lot of emphasis on it.

While the Sun tells us what our inner energy is – what the Chinese call "jin" – the Rising Sign (the Ascendant) tells us how we project ourselves into the world. For example, I know a Gemini Sun person who is so quiet that sometimes I have the urge to smack him upside the head to see if he is still among the living. (That is infinitely more fun that sticking a mirror in front of a person's nose.) Someone like that is an easy target for astro-haters to point to and say, "See, see I told you this is all a bunch of hooey. That person doesn't act at all like a Gemini."

Well, what those smarty-pants don't know is that our semi-comatose Gemini has a very strong Scorpio Ascendant, one of the most restrained of Rising Signs. No, he doesn't ACT like a Gemini – though he devours books like a Gemini but he acts like a secretive, reserved Scorpio because that is his Rising Sign! He is more likely to eat as a Scorpio, as well.

President Obama is a Leo Sun, but has Aquarius as his Rising Sign. All of those people aching to have him be more touchy-feely and a little more emotional are always going to be disappointed. Aquarians love humanity in general but remain detached from people on a one-to-one basis. They are just not emotional beings. Again, we show more of our Rising Sign traits than our Sun Sign traits because Rising Signs are keys to our outward personality.

OK, I can hear you say, "What do you mean by Rising Sign – what is rising, where?" Fair enough.

When the ancients composed the astrological chart system, they based it on twelve houses. Why twelve? Well, it is one of those mystical numbers – there are twelve tribes of Israel, twelve disciples, the ancient Zoroastrians had twelve commanders of light and there were twelve gods on Mount Olympus and so on. Twelve is a number with magical vibrations. Thus we have twelve houses of the Zodiac. (See the chart on page 8.)

Each house contains an energy that corresponds to an area of life. The first is called the Rising Sign because it is on the eastern horizon – where the Sun "rises." On the cusp (or that thin outer wheel) of each house is a sign. It is the energy of that sign and any planets or asteroids that inhabited the actual house at the time of your birth that influence that area of your life.

Because we project as our Rising Sign we are going to eat like our Rising Sign.

The 6th house is the house of health and how we take care of our body, so we have to honor what is there and eat to make us healthy. As I said before, the 4th house is also a "foodie" house. It vibrates to motherly Cancer and tells us how we like to entertain and generally welcome people into our abode.

You can get as general or as specific as you want. The idea is to play with it and have fun!

nodally speaking

Chapter 2

I am an evolutionary or karmic Astrologer. I walk my clients through their past lives and see where they may have some blockages that are keeping them stuck in thinking and actions that just don't work for them anymore. We also explore this life and where they need to be going to get the most out of this incarnation.

Keys to this work are the Nodes, these little invisible marks on the Moon. You know how the Earth goes around the Sun on its invisible axis? Well the Moon also dances on the ecliptic around the Sun as it goes around the Earth. The Nodes are invisible points where the Moon crosses this ecliptic.

Astrologically speaking, the South Node is where we are coming from – past life-wise; the North Node is where we should be progressing in this lifetime. It is sort of the universal end zone for each lifetime.

We often exhibit shadow or negative aspects of our South Node sign, particularly if we have spent far too many lifetimes clinging to it. For instance, my South Node is in Gemini. In my younger days I was excessively high strung, impatient and subject to acid stomach. I sought to consume lots of books – not understand or appreciate them – just get through them or parts of them as fast as I could. These are some of the shadowy aspects of Gemini. I needed in this lifetime to move toward my Sagittarius North Node – to learn and speak my own truth, to become more focused in my learning and to open up to the many spiritual possibilities of the world. (Gemini and Sagittarius are opposite signs. I will explain more below.)

So how does this all relate to food? Simple. When fully in my Gemini, I wanted to eat fast and never ventured into any food area I considered odd. As a kid I always ordered club sandwiches for lunch and Chicken Chow Mein in a Chinese restaurant and meat loaf everywhere else. Why? Because I liked them and didn't want to waste time trying to figure out if I liked something new. Gotta keep moving!

Now as I grow into my North Node, Sagittarius, I appreciate foods of every country (except I can't do Indian; I must have had some wicked past lives in India.)

I love to explore new foods and appreciate enjoying and, of course, making a good meal.

Don't get me wrong. There is nothing wrong with Gemini's *per se* nor is there anything "wrong" with the South Node. It is simply that the universe doesn't want us to keep repeating what we have already learned, so our South Node doesn't fit anymore in this lifetime. Why go back to school and keep repeating the fourth grade? If you are going to go through all the energy and aggravation of reincarnating you might as well move on. The South Node is what we are used to – and some, well many, people get stuck in it, trying to relive what worked before. That is what builds the shadow aspects.

As promised, here is more on the opposite signs of the Astrological wheel. Astrological signs exist in polarity. Because Astrology is built on a wheel system – a circle of 360 degrees – a sign on one side of the chart has a counterpart sign. The signs complement one another. Here is a list of the signs that exist across the wheel and complement each other.

Aries – Libra

Taurus – Scorpio

Gemini – Sagittarius

Cancer- Capricorn

Leo – Aquarius

Virgo – Pisces

Because I come from a Gemini South Node I am moving to the counterpart sign, Sagittarius.

Knowing where a person is coming from and going toward will really help round out their astrological food profile. The further they progress into their North Node, the more they will leave behind their old eating habits.

This movement only applies to the Nodes – not any other placement of the Zodiac. For instance, were I born with Gemini as my Rising Sign, I would not be working on changing that into Sagittarius.

So we have the Sun, the Rising Sign, the 4th and 6th houses and the Nodes ready and hungrily waiting.

Let's get cooking!

aries

Chapter 3

The archetype of Aries is the warrior god; it is the epitome of raw masculine energy. Aries is ruled by Mars and is energetically tied to the 1st house, the house which indicates more than any other how we project our essence into the world. Aries is symbolized by the head-butting ram.

Positive aspects of Aries include:
initiative, action, progress, energy and focused motion.

Shadow aspects of Aries include:
impatience, self-centeredness, anger, immaturity, violence, stubbornness and the need to dominate.

Foodie aspects of Aries include:
a love of the hot, spicy and fast and being a bit of a carnivore.

Famous People with Aries Rising*

Rudolph Valentino – This great early screen heart-throb was purported to love his pasta sauce hot and spicy. While that may have been some movie studio spin to make the sex symbol seem even hotter, it would fit with his Aries rising.

Joan Rivers – She has that talkative Gemini Sun but that Aries rising drive helped her overcome many setbacks including her husband's suicide. She is known to say she doesn't want anything to do with cooking and prefers to make the money to allow other people to cook for her. This is not surprising. How could she like to cook? Gemini is always moving and Aries is too impatient and eager to take on the role as the dominant provider.

*I chose to show Rising Signs instead of Sun Signs because they get less "press" and I feel they are more valuable than Sun Signs. However, you can use these sections to find recipes for people with the sign either in the Sun, or the rising position, or on any of the cusps I have mentioned before (4th and 6th houses) or as a South Node.

Appetizer

Moroccan Braewats

– (sort of)

Aries hate to be bored and they despise having to be seated for too long. Being of the rather demanding temperament, Aries might just stop by at a moment's notice and insist on getting some food. This appetizer can be prepared in advance and later cooked to quickly appease the most agitated son or daughter of Mars.

Braewats are like Moroccan egg rolls. They are traditionally served in dough called wraga but that can be hard to find, so I substituted phyllo. If you are a very patient Virgo cooking for an Aries you will have the ability to wrap the phyllo dough and make a lovely packet. If you are a cook with lots of Aries in your chart, however, you won't have the patience for any of that. You don't have to allow that quick temperament to deprive you of this yummy dish! Just wrap the meat in leaves of lettuce and race off to conquer the world. (The lettuce idea is also good for any sign looking to reduce simple carbs in their diet.)

One of the great things about this dish – besides the taste – is that it can be made as quickly or as slowly as you wish. The lettuce wrap option is quick and very easy.

2–3 tablespoons extra-virgin olive oil
1 medium onion, chopped
2 garlic cloves, chopped
1 ½ pounds ground beef or lamb
½ cup red wine
½ teaspoon paprika
½ stick butter, melted
¼ cup extra-virgin olive oil, (This is not needed if you bake, rather than fry, the Braewats. For baking you will just need some olive oil cooking spray and a tablespoon extra-virgin olive oil.)

½ teaspoon sumac* (see note on page 20)
½ teaspoon chili powder
¾ teaspoon cumin
½ teaspoon cinnamon
½ teaspoon ground ginger
½ teaspoon each kosher salt and freshly ground black pepper
2 teaspoons toasted sesame seeds

For lettuce wraps: (for impatient Air Sign types) 12 medium Bibb lettuce leaves, washed and patted dry
For phyllo wraps: (for the patient Earth Sign types) ½ package phyllo dough

Serves 6

In a large sauté pan heat 2 tablespoons of the oil over low heat. Add the onion and garlic and cook until soft and lightly browned – about 3–4 minutes. Add the beef or lamb and cook until it is begins to brown – about 5 minutes. Add the wine and spices and stir well. Simmer over low heat until the wine is absorbed. Remove from heat and let meat cool to room temperature.

If you are wrapping the meat in lettuce, spoon it into the leaves, fold over into a little packet and serve immediately.

For phyllo wraps, if the phyllo is frozen follow the directions on the package for thawing. It is best to thaw overnight in the refrigerator. Phyllo dries out quickly so read the directions on the package if you have never worked with it before. It can be a bit tricky.

Cut the phyllo into a long strip, 6 inches long and 4 inches wide. Brush the surface with the melted butter. Add about 3 tablespoons of the beef mixture to the end closest to you. Fold over the 2 long side pieces once and then start to fold the strip from the meat side to almost the other end. Just before you reach the end, brush it with butter and fold it over to make a nice sealed packet.

The phyllo packets can be frozen until ready to use. If frozen, bring to room temperature before frying.

To fry, heat ¼ cup of olive oil in a heavy skillet. When the oil is hot, gently place the packets into the oil with a spoon and cook until golden brown, turning to get all sides. Remove with a slotted spoon to a platter lined with paper towels. Drain, sprinkle on the sesame seeds, and serve immediately.

If you are trying to cut down on the fried food, they can be easily baked. Preheat the oven to 375 degrees. Place the Braewats on a greased cookie sheet. Brush the tops lightly with the oil, sprinkle on sesame seeds and bake about 12 minutes until they are golden brown. Serve immediately.

♈ ♉ ♊ ♋ ♌ ♍ ♎ ♏ ♐ ♑ ♒ ♓

Soup

Roasted Tomato Gazpacho Soup

This is a little summery morsel that I came up with when I substituted the tomatoes I roast every summer for the canned tomatoes or even catsup (Jupiter save us) that are often called for in gazpacho recipes. The roasted taste of the tomatoes really gives this a wonderful kick that the Aries will appreciate.

1 large white onion (use red onion if you want a bigger kick), roughly cut
1 cucumber, seeded but not peeled, roughly cut
2 medium red bell peppers, seeded and roughly cut
2–3 fresh jalapeno peppers (don't rub your eyes after you touch these)
3 cups roasted tomatoes (see below) or 2 28-ounce cans crushed tomatoes
    seasoned with basil, oregano and parsley (try to find the fire roasted kind)
4 garlic cloves, minced
1 teaspoon kosher salt

Serves 4 – 6

Working in batches, pulse the onion, cucumber, and the peppers in a food processor until they are small but not mushy. Remove them to a large bowl.

Put the tomatoes in the food processor and run until they are smooth – this won't take long. Remove them to the bowl and add the garlic and salt. Stir well.

Cover and place in the refrigerator for at least 3 hours – overnight is better. The longer it sits the more flavors it absorbs.

For a real bite sprinkle some of the chopped jalapeno on top of each bowl at serving time.

A note on sumac: I learned the beauty of sumac from my friend Susan Kraft. I slip it into a lot of hearty dishes. Just ¼ - ½ a teaspoon really adds a wonderful depth of flavor.

Roasted Tomatoes!

Every summer I take one or two weekends and head to the farmers market with one specific goal – that is – to find as many second tomatoes as I can. These are often tomatoes that are bruised or damaged in some way as to make them less appealing to the spoiled American consumer. The farmers will sell these in bulk at a cheaper price. I get several bushels and head home for a day of roasting. In the winter it is great to make soups and sauces from these wonderful remnants of summer.

5 pounds fresh tomatoes
¼ cup extra-virgin olive oil
3 tablespoons kosher salt
5 tablespoons fresh oregano, chopped

5 tablespoons fresh flat-leaf Italian parsley, chopped
3 tablespoons freshly ground black pepper
1 cup fresh basil leaves

Makes about 3 cups

Preheat the oven to 250 degrees.

Pour the tomatoes into the sink or a large basin filled with cool water for a nice bath. When washed, core and remove any major blemishes. Don't skin them – there is a lot of taste in those skins!

Cover the bottom of a roasting pan with a quarter of an inch of olive oil. Place a single layer of tomatoes in the roasting pan – don't heap them in – even if you have to use several pans just make 1 layer per pan.

Sprinkle the tomatoes with the herbs and spices except for the basil.

Turn the tomatoes with a large spoon – or for more fun, with your hands – until they are coated with the oil and spices. (Touchy-feely Taurus types will like the feel of the tomatoes; imperious Leo and finicky Virgo will be rushing for spoons or gloves or both.) If they seem dry, pour some more oil on top. You don't want them swimming but you want them coated well.

Place the roasting pan into your oven and let them slow cook for 2–3 hours. The tomatoes should be just starting to shrivel. Once they are cool, add the basil leaves to the pan and stir well.

Place the tomatoes with the oil and herbs still in the pan in plastic containers and freeze until the depths of winter or whenever you want the wonderful taste of summer tomatoes.

Pasta

Sausage and Pepper Pasta

Growing up with Italian American parents I was destined to have my fill of pasta, for which I will be eternally grateful. I love pasta. I have included my Mom's pasta sauce recipe – or "gravy" as we used to say in New Jersey below.

Use that sauce for this dish but punch it up for Aries with some sausage and peppers. Make the sauce before you start this recipe.

You can cut the sausage into bite-sized pieces for the impatient Ram.

If you are lucky enough to have a great butcher ask them for a batch of their spiciest sausage. If not, get some spicy Italian sausage at your grocery store, it works too.

5 cups Mom's pasta sauce (see page 24 for recipe)
3–6 tablespoons extra-virgin olive oil, divided
3 garlic cloves, finely chopped
2 large white onions, diced
3 large red bell peppers, seeded and diced

Serves 6

3 pounds spicy Italian sausage,
    cut into ½ inch pieces
3 tablespoons kosher salt
1 pound rigatoni pasta
½ cup ricotta cheese

Remember to make Mom's pasta sauce first. Keep it warming on the stove over low heat. Stir occasionally as it can stick.

Heat 3 tablespoons of the olive oil in a large frying pan over medium heat. Add the garlic and sauté until soft but not brown. Remove from the pan to a small bowl and then add the onions and peppers to the pan; sauté over a medium heat until they get soft – about 8–10 minutes. They might need a little more olive oil. Remove to the same bowl as the garlic.

Sauté the sausage cooking 2–3 minutes on each side until each side is golden brown. Lower the heat and return the onions, garlic and peppers, stir and simmer over low heat.

Bring 6 quarts of water, 1 tablespoon of olive oil and the salt to a boil in a large saucepan. Don't be afraid to salt pasta water – pasta likes salt. When the water boils, add the rigatoni and cook for about 6–8 minutes. Please don't make mush out of your pasta – who wants to eat a pile of boiled wheat?

Bring the heat under the sauce up to medium and bring the sauce to a low boil.

Drain the cooked pasta in a colander over the sink and immediately add it to the pot with the sauce. Add the sausage and vegetables from the frying pan. Stir gently until the pasta, sausage and veggies are married well – but don't smash the pasta or break the sausage. Control that Aries urge to smash! You can ladle the sauce on top on the pasta and not mix it all together. It looks better but I like it mixed up.

Spoon the pasta into the serving bowl and add a dollop of ricotta on top – and some basil if you are feeling fancy.

Serve immediately with any extra sauce on the side.

Jean Garofalo Porte's "Gravy" Sauce

5 tablespoons extra-virgin olive oil
1 white onion, diced
4 garlic cloves, peeled and thinly sliced
3 tablespoons fresh thyme leaves, chopped
2 tablespoons fresh oregano, stemmed and chopped
1 28-ounce can chopped tomatoes,
    or 3 cups roasted tomatoes (see page 21)*
1 teaspoon kosher salt
1 teaspoon sugar
Pinch red pepper flakes
½ cup fresh basil, gently chopped

Serves 6 – 8

In a medium saucepan, over medium heat, warm the olive oil. Add the onion and garlic and sauté until they are browned – about 8–10 minutes. Add the herbs, tomatoes, salt, sugar and pepper. Bring to a boil, while stirring often. If you are going to add meat or eggs, (see page 25) do it while you are bringing the sauce to a boil. Reduce the heat back to medium-low and simmer for about 30 minutes, stirring often. Add the basil.

Sauce can be kept in the refrigerator for 3–4 days and is easily frozen. (I wouldn't recommend freezing sauce with eggs in it. Eggs can freeze but I don't like their texture when thawed.)

*If you are using the roasted tomatoes, pulse them in a food processor until smooth.

You can make a meatless version or sauté a pound of ground beef or veal in a tablespoon of olive oil and then add it to the sauce and let it simmer with the tomatoes. Actually, the best sauces were made when Mom would find a pork chop or spare rib in the refrigerator and add it to the gravy.

My personal favorite would be when she hard boiled some eggs, shelled them and added them to the sauce. This is an acquired taste but I still love eggs in pasta sauce. In fact, since I have gone more "low-carb", eggs in pasta sauce is one way I get my pasta cravings taken care of. The eggs and sauce are very satisfying and take away the need for the pasta.

Veggies & Fruit
Roasted Beets and Carrots

We have to give the sign ruled by the red planet, Mars, something bright red. If you live near a farmers market you can get fresh beets spring, summer and fall. With fresh beets you get the beet greens too, which are yummy and really dress this plate up!

I admit roasting beets takes a while, which may not appeal to an impatient Aries but it isn't like you have to stand there and watch them in the oven to make them cook for goodness sakes. Toss them in, set the timer and go off and stir up some trouble. Besides, they are red and you like red Aries, yes, so stop stamping your feet and try this! A caution about beets – they do tend to stain your hands and clothes so have some good soap and don't make this in your ball gown!

The carrots add color and taste contrast.

12 medium red beets, washed and trimmed
(save the beet greens)
12 medium fresh carrots, washed and scraped
(get rid of the carrot tops unless you are addicted to bitter)
5 tablespoons extra-virgin olive oil, divided
3 tablespoons balsamic vinegar

½ tablespoon each kosher salt and
    freshly ground black pepper
3 tablespoons fresh flat-leaf Italian parsley,
    minced, divided
1 large white onion, chopped
2 garlic cloves, minced

Serves 6

Preheat the oven to 400 degrees.

Place the beets and carrots in a roaster. Pour in 4 tablespoons of the olive oil and all of the vinegar making sure to cover each veggie. Sprinkle with salt and pepper and 2 tablespoons of the parsley. Stir – or for more fun mix them with your hands. Be careful, don't mash them Aries – just be sure every veggie is coated with oil, vinegar and herbs. Roast 45 minutes – be sure they are nicely browned.

Fifteen minutes before the veggies are done wash the beet greens and dice them. Don't use the stem – it is too hard.

Heat a medium sauté pan over medium heat and add 1 tablespoon of the oil. Add the onion and cook for about 5 minutes until soft – add the garlic and cook another minute. Add the beet greens and more salt and pepper if needed. Cook about 15 minutes until the greens are soft.

Place the greens on the serving plate, place the warm beets and carrots on top and sprinkle with the remaining parsley. Serve immediately.

Spicy Corn Pudding

I came to corn pudding relatively late in life and it has become one of my favorites. Yes, this will taste better with fresh corn, but if you are the Aries (or an impatient Air Sign like Gemini) doing the cooking you will buy canned corn. (Don't deny it. I see it in your stars.) No worries. That will work too.

Because this is adapted from a Native American recipe, this will appeal to the little kid in Aries. They are the first sign and called the children of the Zodiac. This will take them back to their childhood and stories like "The Last of the Mohicans."

3 tablespoons extra-virgin olive oil
4 shallots, diced
¼ cup poblano peppers, seeded and diced
¼ cup red peppers, diced
3 garlic cloves, minced
1 teaspoon kosher salt
¼ teaspoon cayenne pepper
1 teaspoon fresh flat-leaf Italian parsley, diced
2 cups fresh corn (or 1 15-ounce can of corn)

1 ½ cups half and half
3 eggs
¼ cup all-purpose flour (If you prefer wheat flour or have to use gluten free substitutes, fine; just add about another ¼ cup half and half as they can be dryer than white)
¾ cup grated cheese (If you really want a kick use a pepper jack or other peppery cheese; if not, a Munster or Havarti would work. I used Gouda once and it worked fine)
2 slices red pepper, for decoration

Serves 6 – 8

Preheat the oven to 375 degrees.

Heat the olive oil in a medium sauté pan over medium heat; add the shallots and peppers and cook about 5 minutes until soft. Add the garlic and cook another minute. Remove everything to a medium bowl off the heat. Add the salt, pepper and parsley to the pan and stir. Add the corn and cook for about 6 minutes, until it starts to brown. Remove these to the same medium bowl.

In a large bowl whisk the half and half and eggs until combined well.

Place the corn mixture and flour in the food processor and pulse until well mixed. Continue to pulse as you pour the half and half/egg mixture in slowly until well blended and the flour is totally incorporated.

Pour the mixture into a well greased 1-quart casserole. Sprinkle the cheese over the top and bake for 50 minutes. The top should be golden brown. Just before serving decorate the top with the red pepper slices.

A note on freezing corn: It is easy to bring another wonderful taste of summer to winter. Husk the corn and blanch quickly in a pot of boiling water. Remove the corn, cool, dry and place in plastic bags. Seal well and freeze.

Meat & Fish

Jerry Anderson's Elk Stew

I went to my old friend Jerry Anderson who lives in Texas for this one. Aries is the epitome of raw, masculine energy and what appeals more to the traditional masculine sensibility than hunting your own food?

You don't have to be a hunter to make this. If you can't find elk or bison at your specialty food store, heck, substitute a rump or sirloin beef roast. Do try to get elk; however, it is very low in fat and quite tasty.

2 pounds elk, cubed (all fat, bone and sinew removed)
½ cup all-purpose flour
4 tablespoons extra-virgin olive oil
1 large white onion, peeled and wedged
3 garlic cloves, minced
2 teaspoons kosher salt
½ teaspoon freshly ground black pepper
1 4-inch sprig of fresh rosemary, chopped
6 tablespoons fresh flat-leaf Italian parsley, minced

Serves 6 – 8

2 celery stalks, diced
2 carrots, diced
1 cup white potatoes, quartered
½ cup crushed tomatoes
1 cup red wine
1 tablespoon paprika
6 cups of chicken or beef stock (see page 44)
1 cup green beans (frozen, fresh or canned)
1 baguette French bread, thickly sliced

Dredge the meat in the flour. In a large sauté pan, over medium heat, add the olive oil and cook the onion until it starts to get translucent – about 5–8 minutes; add the garlic and cook another 2 minutes. Remove the onion and garlic to a medium bowl.

Add the meat to the pan and cook until it is well seared on all sides – about 2 minutes per side. Add all of the ingredients except the bread to the pan. Simmer for 1 hour allowing liquid to reduce by half.

Serve immediately over a slice of the French bread.

A note on wine: I don't get all fussy about wine. Use the wine you like to drink – you have to eat the food so it should be steeped in the wine you enjoy. Do not use cooking wine – it is creepy and full of salt.

Stuffed Peppers

My Mom made great stuffed peppers. That is funny for me to say because I hate peppers especially the green ones. I would eat the stuffing and slip her the pepper – she was addicted to them. Your Aries shouldn't have a problem with peppers but if you want a sweeter taste, substitute red for green peppers. Besides, red is the color of Mars and Aries!

If you are of the anti-pepper crowd, core out some summer squash or zucchini and use them instead. They work just as well.

I have modernized her recipe a bit but the basics are Mom's.

These are also a great do-ahead dish as you can freeze the peppers and then pop them into the oven when you want to eat them. That is another benefit for the impetuous Aries.

2 tablespoons extra-virgin olive oil
2 white onions, diced
3 garlic cloves, diced
1 teaspoon fresh oregano, minced
2 teaspoons fresh thyme, minced
2 teaspoons fresh flat-leaf Italian parsley, minced
2 teaspoons kosher salt
2 teaspoons freshly ground black pepper
1 pound ground beef or pork or a combination of the two (You can do ground turkey if you want to be healthy – just add more spices than you would if using beef, as turkey is a bit taste deprived.)

1 ½ cups red wine, divided
1 ½ cups cooked rice – brown is fine and better for you
2 cups cooked baby spinach, finely chopped
6 whole red or green peppers
1 32 ounce can tomato sauce
1-2 cups red wine
1 loaf thick Italian bread, sliced

Serves 6

In a large sauté pan heat the oil over medium heat. Cook the onions and garlic until they are soft – about 3–4 minutes. Add the spices and stir. Add the meat and cook until well browned – about 5 minutes. Pour in ½ cup of the wine

In a large bowl mix the rice and spinach, then stir into the meat mixture. Cook another 3 minutes then remove from heat.

Wash the peppers, take off the tops and remove the seeds. Stuff the peppers with the meat and rice mixture. Aries, please be gentle, you don't want to tear the peppers or make big gashes in them.

The peppers can be frozen at this point.

In a large soup or stock pot place the peppers upright in the pan –don't crowd them; you want them to cook all around. Pour the tomato sauce and 1 cup of wine around the peppers. The liquid should be about ¾ the way up on the peppers – don't drown them. You may have to add more wine or you may have to cut back.

Cover the pot and cook over low heat for 45 minutes. Periodically check to be sure they are not burning. You may have to add more liquid. The peppers are done when they begin to wrinkle.

If you are using squash or zucchini instead of peppers you can lay them flat in the pot and cook for 35–40 minutes. Again, be gentle; you don't want to end up with a mashed up pile of veggies and meat. Yes, I am talking to you Fire Signs, Aries, Leo and Sagittarius, and even you impatient Air Signs.

Carefully remove the peppers onto a serving plate and spoon the tomato sauce over top. Serve this immediately with a nice Italian bread to sop up the sauce.

A note on salt and pepper: I always prefer kosher or sea salt – try both if you have never used either and see which you prefer. Freshly ground black peppercorns are much better than the canned stuff. Get a little grinder and some peppercorns and see what I mean.

To Their Health

Pastina with Mint Pesto

People with Aries on the cusp of the 6th house (the house of health) and strong Aries Ascendants and Suns or a strong Mars influence in their charts can run high fevers. (They are also prone to smacking the heck out of their heads because they charge off without looking, but food can't help that too much.)

I can't do much for the head but I can help soothe the fevers. Mint is a very cooling food that is easy to grow. Actually, it is too easy. Don't ever plant mint in anything but a container because if it gets in the ground it will take over everything else like the monster that ate Cleveland.

One of the throw-backs to my childhood is the memory of pastina when I wasn't feeling well. Pastina means "little pasta." When I was growing up in Northern New Jersey you could get Ronzoni pastina, which is still one of the best. You might have to search for pastina depending on where you live – or you can always substitute orzo or any other small pasta.

The mint pesto can be made at the height of the summer season and frozen.

½ cup Mint Pesto (If you want to make it
  yourself, see below)
1 tablespoon butter
1 small white onion, diced
2 cups peas, canned or frozen

1 pound pastina (or other small pasta)
2 tablespoons kosher salt
2 teaspoons freshly ground black pepper
¼ cup fresh Parmigiano-Reggiano cheese, shaved

Serves 4

Make (see below) or defrost the mint pesto.

In a small saucepan heat the butter over low heat, add the onion and sauté about 5–6 minutes until it begins to look translucent. Add the peas and stir well until peas are warmed thoroughly.

Cook the pastina in a large soup pot of boiling salted water (about 3 quarts) for about 6 minutes. I don't like to squish my pasta – think *al dente*. Drain the pasta in a colander over the sink and place it into a large serving bowl. Immediately stir in the pesto and peas. Season with the pepper and then taste for salt and adjust if you have to.

Shave some fresh Parmigiano-Reggiano cheese over the top before serving. Yes, you can cheat and shake some of the canned stuff over it but it won't taste nearly as good, I promise.

Mint Pesto

This is a basic recipe for all pestos. You can substitute the mint for basil or other herbs. Spinach, parsley and kale also make great pestos.

  1 cup fresh mint leaves
  2 tablespoons pine nuts*
  2 tablespoons Parmigiano-Reggiano or Romano cheese,
    freshly grated
  1 cup extra-virgin olive oil

  Makes about ½ cup.

Place everything but the olive oil in the food processor. As you start the processor slowly pour in the olive oil. Keep processing until the mixture is very fine.

You can pour the pesto in plastic containers and freeze.

*A note on nuts: I am not allergic to pine nuts but I know people who are. However, I do have a nut allergy. (Pine nuts are not really nuts but seeds.) You can replace the pine nuts with chopped walnuts but for heaven's sakes tell people what you have put in the pesto. A swollen, itchy Aries is not a sign you want to behold.

Opposites Attract: Stretching Your Aries South Node

The sign opposite Aries is Libra. If you read the chapter on the North and South Nodes, you know that if you have Aries on the South Node you are moving to a more Libra direction in this lifetime (or should be!) Where Aries is the warrior, concerned with getting things done for their own benefit, Libra is all about the other person. Aries is all about "Look at me go do and conquer" and Libra is "Let us share and have lunch." I may have taken a bit of liberty with a deep mystical alignment but you get my drift.

Try this Hot Pot Recipe for any highly Aries person. It will appeal to the warrior in Aries but is a great dish to share with others and if there is one thing Aries needs to learn, it is how to share.

Aries Hot Pot

If you are an Aries cook the last thing you want to do is wait around for your food to simmer slowly. You want things fast – you want them to be there when you want them to be there! The Hot Pot is sometimes called the Mongolian Hot Pot, the legend being that Mongolian warriors cooked their food in their helmets while on military escapades. Personally I can't see Genghis and the boys hopping off their yaks or whatever to cook up a savory stew in their helmets. I mean, we are not talking helmets made out of "space age steel" here, and while I am not a military strategist it doesn't make too much sense to me. Can you image being ambushed and not being able to protect yourself because your hats are boiling hot over the fire? However, it is a good myth that appeals to the warrior blood of the Aries. Because of that and the Aries' primal fascination with cooking the food at the table, I have dubbed this recipe the Aries Hot Pot. (You can almost hear them say, "I am Aries. I like fire. I like watching my catch being cooked in front of me.")

If you are cooking for an Aries and they are not breathing down your neck so you have some time to prepare, you can go with the meat version because it takes a bit more time. If they are butting you with their ram horns, stick with the fish version.

Hot Pots can be made in fondue pots or even regular stainless steel or aluminum pots. If you use non-electric pots you will need to keep a large pot of stock boiling on the stove to reheat the serving pots.

It is best to have one pot for every four people.

3 tablespoons extra-virgin olive oil

4 slices fresh ginger, thinly sliced

2 garlic cloves, diced

1 ½ quarts beef stock

1 bottle white wine

2 pounds beef eye round or pork shoulder or one of each.*

2 pounds baby spinach (or cabbage), washed

6 ounces white button mushrooms, cleaned. (The smaller the better, if you can only get big ones just cut them in half.)

1 pound baby corn (If you can't find small corn cut a few cobs in half after they are shucked and washed)

Your favorite dipping sauces

Serves 4

*I like beef or pork, although lamb can be used. (Frankly I have seen some recipes with animals in them I have never heard of but I haven't made any of those! So tap into Aries adventurism and use whatever meat you like. Just be sure it is cut paper thin.)

Heat the oil in a large stock pot over medium-high heat. Add the ginger and garlic and sauté until the garlic goes soft – about a minute or two.

Add the stock and wine to the pot and raise heat to medium-high. Once it begins to boil turn it down to simmer until you are ready to cook.

Slice the meat paper thin. (If you can't get a butcher to do this, stick the meat in the freezer for about an hour before you cut it; your knife will thank you for it.)

Bring the stock back up to a strong boil and carefully ladle into your serving pot to just under ¾ full. Don't overfill as it will spill over when you add the food. Remember if the serving pot isn't electric, keep some stock simmering on the stove to warm it while eating.

At the table drop the veggies and meat in the hot pot and cook for about 3–4 minutes. The thinner the meat the faster it will cook.

Have ladles for people to fish out their food or put serving bowls out and serve up dishes.

With all of the wonderful sauces on the market there is no need to make your own. A simple soy sauce will do; hot mustards are wonderful condiments, and ginger soys are great too. Place as many condiment bowls out as you like and have fun with your food.

For a Fish Hot Pot

    1 pound medium shrimp, peeled and deveined
    1 pound scallops, cleaned

Make the stock above only using fish stock instead of beef. Fill your hot pots with the boiling fish stock just as you would do for the meat.

There is no cutting necessary – just toss the scallops and then the shrimp into the hot pots at the table. Scallops should cook about 5–6 minutes, the shrimp about 2 minutes. Serve with dipping sauces.

Dessert

Grilled Coconut Chocolate Fruit

This is fun and sloppy – a perfect dessert for the baby of the Zodiac. (Aries is the first sign of the Zodiac and vibrates to the 1st house so it is often called the baby. When Aries doesn't get their way they often cry and stamp their feet like babies!) For me it is reminiscent of those coconutty- chocolate patties we used to get in Florida when we visited my grandparents and I could devour by the ton as a kid! (Ah youth!) You can grill almost any fruit; pineapples, pears, apples and peaches are the norm. You can also use bananas (just keep the heat low) or watermelon. You can use any combination, really. For six people I use one sliced medium pineapple and three sliced pears, apples, bananas or peaches. One half watermelon sliced into triangles will do. Again, you can mix and match – take two pears and ½ a pineapple if you prefer – the fruit is up to you. Try mangos or oranges if you like them. You should have about three cups of fruit for six people. Have some lemons on hand. Apples and pears go brown quickly when cut unless you squeeze some fresh lemon juice over them.

Have fun!

Grilling Fruit

    Fruit – see above
    Juice of 4 medium lemons
    3 tablespoons honey
    1 ½–2 cups shredded coconut
    If using bananas – bamboo sticks or long toothpicks

    Serves 6

Chocolate Sauce

    12 ounces semisweet chocolate chips
    ½ cup milk

Combine the chocolate and milk in a double boiler and cook over medium heat until the chocolate is melted and blended with the milk. Take off the heat but leave the mixture in the top of the boiler.

If you are using a charcoal grill make a low flame – for a gas grill – turn on medium heat. You don't want to scorch the fruit. Place ¼ cup of water, lemon juice and honey in a small saucepan and heat over medium heat until the honey is melted– about 5 minutes. Take off the heat and cool 5 minutes.

For everything except bananas cut the fruit and place into the water/honey mixture for 20 minutes before putting on the grill. For the bananas it is best to put them on the fire in their peels and then shuck and slice them later.

Grill the fruit until they have nice grill marks and are just lightly caramelized. Take them off the grill and place on a large serving platter.

If the chocolate sauce has become too thick, just place over the heat again and add a few drops of milk until it loosens. With a pastry brush apply the sauce to one side of the fruit. Immediately sprinkle the coconut over the chocolate sauce. Don't let the chocolate sauce harden –put the coconut on right away.

For bananas, shuck from the peel, slice into bite-size pieces, place them on the toothpicks and then dip into the chocolate and roll in coconut that has been placed on waxed paper.

Let the fruit cool and the sauce harden before serving.

You don't need ice cream for this – but if you want to serve with ice cream – have at it!

A note on lemons: A warm lemon yields more juice than a cold one. Roll it between your hands for a few minutes or pop into the microwave for about 5–10 seconds – no more!

Famous People
with
Aries South Node –
Libra North Node

Madonna –

Yes, I guess you can say she is someone who came in with a bunch of past lives where she was dominant, forceful and wanting to be the center of attention. Every time she seems to be fading from the music charts, she will do something outrageous to get back on the front pages. That is very indicative of the "pay attention to me' demand made by many people used to being an Aries. She admitted to David Letterman that, despite living in New York for many years, she never got around to sampling New York pizza. Of course not, she is too Aries – always rushing around and missing what is under her nose.

Sarah Ferguson –

A wee bit headstrong, yes, and Sarah also displays another trait left over from her days as an Aries, which is the absolute refusal to listen to people. She has to keep slamming her Aries head into the wall doing things that she will later regret, much like a child putting her hand in a hot flame when all of the adults are yelling stop. Her famous battles with her weight are frankly due more to having Jupiter, the planet of expansion, in her 1st house. However, I find it very Aries of her to tout a white bean dip as one of her "go to" recipes. It is fast and easy and can be eaten on the fly.

In a 1967 interview Aries rising Barbra Streisand claimed that she has adored spicy
Chinese food from her early teens. Very Aries of you, Ms. Streisand!

taurus
Chapter 4

Where Aries is all male, the archetype of Taurus is the beautiful, feminine epicure. Ruled by Venus and energetically tied to the 2nd house Taurus likes tactile beauty and warm, comfortable, safe surroundings. The 2nd house indicates how we seek to make ourselves safe and secure in the world. It is the house of stability.

Positive aspects of Taurus include:
being a lover and creator of beauty, financial stability, strength of character and sensuality.

Shadow aspects of Taurus include:
gluttony, stubbornness and hoarding.

Foodie aspects of Taurus include:
a love of the rich, comforting foods that appeal to the touch as well as to the palate.

Taureans tend to have – well – sturdy bodies and some can get a bit large. It is easy for them to let themselves go. Their symbol is the bull. If you are a Taurus concerned about your ability to gain weight or cooking for one – you can substitute two percent milk for cream and use turkey bacon for regular bacon in the following Taurus recipes. They won't have the mouth-feel Taurus craves but they will make your doctor happier.

Famous People with Taurus Rising

Maria Shriver – She served as a creative director for an ice cream company called "Lovin Scoopful." That is such a Taurus food! Ice cream is creamy, rich and comforting with a great mouth-feel.

Mae West – I love her quote, "The only carrots that interest me are the numbers you get in a diamond." Need I say more? Carrots are just not scrumptious enough to appeal to Taurus. Diamonds, however, are a very different story!

Appetizer
Rosemary -Parmesan Bone Marrow

I know there is a bit of "ewww" factor with bone marrow (I can hear the Virgos shrieking now) but be honest, who hasn't gnawed on a steak bone or sucked on the pork chop bone until the last morsel of meat is off? (Yeah, the Virgos are still shrieking.) When others of us do that we are going for the marrow! It is juicy and luscious and appeals to the tactile and highly sensual Taurus.

6 beef bone marrow bones *
5 tablespoons extra-virgin olive oil, divided
1 baguette of crunchy bread, cut into ¼ inch rounds

¼ cup rosemary leaves, stems removed, finely chopped
¼- ½ pound good hard Parmigiano-Reggiano cheese, thinly sliced

Serves 6

Preheat the oven to 375 degrees.

Cover the bottom of a roasting pan with aluminum foil. Place the marrow bones in the roasting pan. Pour 2–3 tablespoons of the oil over the bones and be sure to turn them to cover well in the oil. Roast for 15–20 minutes until the marrow is soft. When you remove the pan from the oven, cover the top with foil to keep warm.

While the bones are roasting, place the bread on a cookie sheet and spread the remaining oil over top of each with a pastry brush. Place in the oven and cook for 5–8 minutes, until the rounds are crispy and brown. Check them after 3 minutes – you don't want them to burn.

A note on grated cheese: Please buy small hunks of cheese and grind them yourself in the food processor as you need them. Trust me; you will taste the difference in one bite from the stuff in the can.

Shave the cheese thinly with a mandolin, vegetable peeler or paring knife. If you are an accident prone Aries, Sagittarius or Aquarius type do be careful especially with the mandolin. Use the safety protector.

When you remove the bread from the oven sprinkle each slice with the rosemary. Place a slice of cheese on top of each bread round.

Serve the warm marrow with the bread and small spoons or spreaders and the extra sliced cheese on the side. To eat, scoop the marrow on top of the bread.

*Butcher shops have them but if you don't have a butcher shop, ring the bell at the meat section of your grocery store. If they don't have them in stock they can easily get them for you.

Soup

Potato Leek Soup

The creaminess of this soup will appeal to the touchy-feely Taurus. They are the most tactile of the Zodiac and need to feel, wear and, yes, eat things that provide comfort and warmth and are also hearty and filling. Taurus doesn't go much for "frou-frous" foods; they want to know they are eating something of substance. Did you ever try to feed a bull a tiny button mushroom? Good, you would probably have been gored.

2 tablespoons extra-virgin olive oil
7 medium potatoes, peeled and quartered
8 leeks, diced
2 garlic cloves, diced
3 celery stalks, roughly chopped
2 medium onions, peeled and quartered
2 quarts chicken stock (see page 44)

Serves 6 – 8

½ cup white wine
½ cup all purpose flour
6 ounces butter, melted
1 cup heavy cream
2 teaspoons fresh thyme leaves, minced
1 teaspoon kosher salt
1 teaspoon freshly ground black pepper
2 tablespoons fresh chives, minced

Heat the oil in in a large soup pot over medium-low heat. Add the potatoes, leeks, garlic, celery and onions, and sauté until the garlic begins to brown– about 5 minutes. Add the chicken stock and wine and bring to a boil. Allow to boil until the potatoes are soft– about 15–20 minutes; stir often to prevent sticking.

Meanwhile, mix the flour and butter in small bowl. Add this, the cream and spices, except the chives, to the potato mixture and mix until well combined. Remove from the heat and let cool. If you have an immersion blender use it to blend the mixture until smooth. You can also blend in a food processor. Be careful when you blend soup; it is easy to get burned.

Pour the soup back into the pot and simmer over medium-low heat for 20 more minutes until the soup has thickened, stirring often. Pour into a soup tureen or serving bowls, sprinkle with the chives and serve immediately.

Chicken Stock

This makes about two quarts of stock and freezes very well. By roasting the chicken first, you get a much deeper flavor to your stock.

>   3 tablespoons extra-virgin olive oil
>   1 whole chicken, cut up
>   6 celery stalks, roughly chopped
>   6 carrots, roughly chopped
>   3 teaspoons kosher salt
>   1 teaspoon freshly ground black pepper

Preheat the oven to 375 degrees.

Place the oil in a large roasting pan and add the chicken. Roast the chicken for about 60 minutes. Remove from the oven and place in a large soup pot with the rest of the ingredients and pour in 4–5 quarts of water. Simmer over low heat for 4–5 hours. You may have to add more water and you will need to skim off the froth on top from time to time. Take it off the heat and let it cool. Strain the stock through a colander into a large bowl. Throw out the chicken and veggies – they have no more taste left.

Once cold, you can freeze the stock for that fast Gemini soup. I refrigerate it overnight and skim off any remaining fat before freezing.

A note on using fresh products: always – always smell any fresh products. Of course, we test fish and chicken but give everything the sniff – if veggies look wilted and sad – sniff around – if your nose says no toss them into the compost pile. Even oils and vinegars can go rancid. Never keep oils more than a year. Always sniff anything that is fresh before you toss it in. You would hate to toss all of your work out because you added something bad.

Pasta

Baked Pasta Carbonara

Pasta Carbonara is definitely on my last meal list – it is a creamy delight and at that point, hey screw the carbs! Baking it will make the Taurus happier than the on-the-stove type because the house will smell like warm baking cheese. Taurus loves the smell of anything yummy coming from the oven.

10 ounces pancetta, cubed

3 garlic cloves, minced

1 pound penne pasta

4 teaspoons kosher salt

3 cups ricotta cheese (you can use part skim ricotta if your bull is watching his or her weight)

2 large eggs, beaten

2 teaspoons fresh flat-leaf Italian parsley, finely chopped

2 teaspoons fresh thyme, finely chopped

1 teaspoon fresh oregano, finely chopped

½ teaspoon freshly ground black pepper

1 ½ cups mozzarella cheese, grated

1 cup Parmigiano-Reggiano cheese, grated

Serves 6

Preheat the oven to 450 degrees.

In a medium sauté pan cook the pancetta until crispy and drain on a paper towel. Add the garlic to the pan and sauté until soft– just about 1 minute. Remove from the heat.

Bring 2-3 quarts of water and salt to a boil over medium-high heat in a large soup pot. Cook the penne pasta for about 6 – 8 minutes. Remember, you want *al dente,* not mush.

While the pasta is cooking mix the ricotta cheese with the eggs, parsley, thyme, oregano, pepper and mozzarella cheese in a large bowl until everything is combined.

Drain the pasta in a colander over the sink, shake off any excess water and then add a little (about 2 tablespoons) of the cheese/egg mixture to the pasta. Shake it around and then immediately put the pasta in the remaining cheese/egg mixture. Mix quickly to stop the eggs from scrambling – make sure the pasta is well coated. Air Signs, pay attention to this – don't let it scramble; Earth Signs, don't mix this to death so the pasta mushes. Follow the Libra and achieve some balance here.

Pour it into a greased 1 quart casserole dish. Top with the Parmigiano-Reggiano cheese.

Bake about 8 minutes until the cheeses turn a golden brown. Serve immediately.

Veggies & Fruit

Tomatoes Stuffed With Artichokes & Feta

Taurus is a bit confusing when it comes to color. Bulls are drawn to the color red; however, the color associated with Taurus is emerald green, symbolizing the pastures in which they love to laze comfortably. Therefore, I offer here a very red veggie dish with a dash of green.

One of the first dishes I made when I was a kid were tomatoes stuffed with chicken and tuna salads. I thought they were just the neatest things. As I grew as a person and a cook, I encountered many recipes that stuffed tomatoes with some kind of creamy spinach messes or ones that were all breadcrumbs and cheese.

This recipe is my grown-up version of the stuffed tomato that embraces the artichoke as well and is easy enough for the sometimes lazy Taurus to make. (Did I say lazy? Oops. I hope they don't stampede.)

6 large firm tomatoes*
1 tablespoon extra-virgin olive oil
2 14-ounce cans un-marinated
   artichoke hearts, diced
3 shallots, diced
3 garlic cloves, diced

Serves 6

Juice of ½ lemon
½ cup pitted Kalamata olives, roughly chopped
1 teaspoon fresh oregano, minced
10 ounces feta cheese, crumbled
6 big basil leaves

Preheat the oven to 350 degrees.

Cut the stems off of the tomatoes and scoop out the pulp, leaving the shell. Set the pulp aside in a small dish. Drain the artichoke hearts in a colander.

Heat the oil in a medium sauté pan over medium heat. Rough chop the tomato pulp and add to the pan; cook down until most of the moisture of the tomato is gone. Add the shallots and garlic and sauté until soft – about 2 minutes. (You may have to drizzle more olive oil into the pan to keep the veggies from sticking.)

Remove the cooked vegetables to a small dish to cool and add the artichoke hearts to the pan. Cook until they begin to turn golden brown. Squeeze the juice of the lemon in a small dish (watch the pits) and pour over the hearts. Let the lemon juice cook down and add the olives.

Stir in the oregano and remove immediately from the heat. Add all of the vegetables together in one dish and let the mixture cool to the touch.

Fill the tomatoes ½ way with artichoke mixture, add a layer of feta, fill the tomato to the top with more artichoke mixture and top with more feta. Place a basil leaf on top of each tomato.

Place tomatoes on a greased cookie sheet and bake for 10 minutes. The cheese should be melted and lightly brown.

Serve warm.

*Depending on the size of your tomatoes you may have some artichokes left over. The mixture is great reheated and used as a topping for steaks or salads.

A note on tomatoes: Please don't buy tomatoes in the winter. They taste like dust and they are picked by people who live in slave-like conditions. No, they are slaves. I suggest that if you care about where your food comes from, read "Tomatoland" by Barry Estabrook

Lobster Cobb Salad

I love Maine and I love lobster – well sort of. I don't like hot lobster. It takes on a bitter taste to me. When I was introduced to Lobster Cobb Salad I fell back in love with the tasty, ugly little creature.

Taurus will like the creaminess of the cheese and avocado and the luxury of the lobster. Arrange the eggs, beans and tomatoes carefully to give your Taurus a perfect meal time experience. They are visually oriented as well as tactile and they are orderly little buggers. Not as orderly as Capricorn or Virgo – but they don't like messes in their little pastures…darn their ruling planet Venus.

If you don't like cooking whole lobsters just buy some fresh claw or tail meat from your local fish monger.

For Salad:

    2 pounds fresh lobster meat, cut into ½ inch pieces.
    6 hard-boiled eggs, shelled and sliced
    ½ pound fresh green beans, trimmed
    2 teaspoons kosher salt
    ½ pound bacon
      (If you want another level of flavor
       try to get apple smoked bacon)
    2 hearts romaine, cut into one inch pieces*
    ½ pound cherry tomatoes, halved
    2 teaspoons freshly ground black pepper
    2 ripe avocados
    ½ lemon, juiced
    4 ounces English Stilton cheese, crumbled

    Serves 6

For Dressing:

Juice of 2 lemons
3 tablespoons Dijon mustard
½ cup extra-virgin olive oil
¼ cup red wine vinegar
1 garlic clove, minced
1 teaspoon kosher salt
2 teaspoons freshly ground black pepper

Whisk together the lemon juice, mustard, olive oil, vinegar, garlic, salt and pepper in a small bowl until smooth.

Cooking lobster is no fun. If you have fresh lobsters, get the big pot on, boil up the water and toss them in. They need to cook about 10 minutes, until the shells turn red. While they are cooking prepare an ice bath – a large bowl filled with ice water and ice. Take them out of the water and place them in the ice water. When cooled, remove the meat from the tail and claws and chop the meat. Keep in the refrigerator until ready to use.

A note on hard boiled eggs: Place the eggs in a saucepan and just barely cover them with water. Once they come back to a boil, turn off the heat and let them sit for 25 minutes. Drain and crack the eggs.

You can also go buy cooked lobster meat. No one will shame and mock you in the streets for goodness' sakes! However, you will lose some taste.

In a medium saucepan over medium-high heat, boil the beans in just enough salted water to cover them, for about 2 minutes. You want them crispy. While they are cooking prepare another ice bath. As soon as the beans are done, drain them in the sink and toss them in the ice bath to shock them, stop the cooking process and keep the crisp green color.

In a medium sauté pan cook the bacon until crisp and set aside to cool. Then crumble into small pieces.

In a large mixing bowl, combine the cooled lobster meat, beans and tomatoes in ½ of the vinaigrette sauce until all are covered. Add the salt and pepper.

Peel, pit and half the avocados, pour the lemon juice over, cover and reserve in a small bowl.

I like making Cobb salad in pretty layers in a glass salad bowl and the Taurus will like the artistic appeal. Place the lettuce on the bottom of the bowl, then layer in the tomatoes then the beans and then the sliced eggs. The next layer is the bacon, followed by the avocados. Arrange the lobster pieces on top and finally the Stilton.

Serve with the rest of the vinaigrette sauce on the side.

*I am not a big fan of arugula but if you like it go for it.

Meat & Fish

Scallops with Mushrooms

I love scallops and I love mushrooms and they make a luxurious combination that is very appealing to the Taurus. Don't get skimpy, wimpy scallops. Remember, you are feeding the bull. Don't tell them this isn't that fattening; it is better to appeal to the glutton in them. This also makes a lovely presentation, – and it is all about the presentation for the Taurus.

½ pound fresh shiitake mushrooms
½ pound oyster mushrooms
½ pound Portobello mushrooms
½ pound button mushrooms
2 tablespoons butter
3 tablespoons extra-virgin olive oil
7 scallions, diced

4 slices fresh ginger
1 teaspoon kosher salt
1 teaspoon freshly ground black pepper
1 cup white wine
16 large sea scallops
1 tablespoon fresh flat-leaf Italian parsley, minced

Serves 4

Gently brush away any dirt on the mushrooms with a dry wad of paper towel. (I know, I am tempted to wash them too. If you are heavy on the Virgo, Leo or Capricorn and must put them in water, do it FAST and don't blame me if you lose some of the taste.)

Slice the mushrooms into long pieces. Place the butter in a medium sauté pan over medium heat and cook the mushrooms, for 5 minutes, or until they are lightly browned on all sides, stirring occasionally. (If you have drowned them in water for cleaning you should put the mushrooms into the pan without the butter and cook over low heat until they start to dry out. Then add the butter and continue to sauté.)

Remove the mushrooms to a plate and add 1 tablespoon of olive oil to the pan. Add the scallions and sauté over medium heat for about 5 minutes until they are lightly brown and getting soft. Add the ginger, salt, pepper and wine and return the mushrooms to the pan. Cook until the wine is almost evaporated, making sure you stir gently to keep them from sticking. Don't smash the mushrooms – be gentle. Think of Venus dancing gently on the mushrooms.

Cook about 10 minutes until the mushrooms are soft. You may have to add more wine. Remove the ginger slices and set the pan aside.

You can prepare the mushrooms up to 3 hours in advance – just reheat them before you add the scallops. You want the scallops to finish cooking with the mushrooms to meld the flavors.

Rinse the scallops carefully to remove any grit. If your scallops have white, sinewy looking pieces on the side smack your fishmonger (kidding, Leo!) and then trim them off with a sharp knife.

Blot the scallops dry with paper towels and season with salt and pepper. In a large sauté pan, brown the scallops in 2 tablespoons of oil over high heat for about 2 minutes. Get a nice light brown on both sides; turn them carefully with a spatula.

Transfer the scallops to the pan with the hot mushrooms. Cover the pan, turn off the heat and let the scallops finish cooking in the residual heat of the pan for about 3 minutes.

Place the scallops on a serving dish, spoon the mushroom mixture around the scallops and sprinkle with chopped parsley and serve.

*If you don't have access to a good farmers market or store that offers a variety of mushrooms you can use cremini mushrooms but try to get some kind of variety as it really enhances the flavor.

Beef Bourguignon

This was a big dish in the '70s that I wish would come back. (Believe me, that is about all I want back from that decade – remember those shoes?) It appeals to Taurus on so many levels, it smells great, and it is creamy and tender and looks luxurious.

Taureans often get the moniker of "lazy bulls." This isn't entirely fair. They are not necessarily lazy; they just don't like to expend too much excess energy if they don't really have to. This recipe is good for the bull who is conserving energy as it almost makes itself in the pot.

½ pound bacon

3 pounds chuck beef, cut into 1-inch cubes

4 teaspoons kosher salt

3 teaspoons freshly ground black pepper

4 garlic cloves, chopped

12 ounces pearl onions

1 pound carrots, diced

1 bottle red wine

3 cups beef stock

¾ teaspoon fresh thyme, diced

¾ teaspoon oregano, diced

2 tablespoons tomato paste

¼ stick butter

1 pound mushroom caps, sliced

¼ cup fresh flat-leaf Italian parsley, finely chopped

Serves 6

Preheat the oven to 250 degrees.

Heat a large Dutch oven on the stove over low heat and cook the bacon until it is crisp. Remove it from the pan and place in a large dish lined with a paper towel. Sprinkle the beef with salt and pepper, and sauté in the same Dutch oven in the bacon fat over medium heat browning on all sides. Remove the beef from the pan and add to the bacon.

In the same pan, sauté the garlic and onions until they are lightly browned and soft. (You may have to add a bit of olive oil depending on how fatty the beef and bacon were.) Remove from the pan and put into the dish with the meat.

Add the carrots to the pan and sauté until soft and lightly browned – about 3 minutes. Turn off the heat.

Put the meat and other veggies back into the pan with the carrots. Pour in the red wine, beef stock and add the spices and tomato paste. Stir well but gently until everything is blended well. Cover and place in the oven for 2–3 hours until the meat is very tender. Check that the wine and stock are still half way up the pan – you may have to add more of either. I will let you decide which!

In a small sauté pan melt the butter and cook the mushrooms until soft and brown – about 5 minutes. Add to the beef mixture, sprinkle with the parsley and serve.

A note on carrots: to peel or not to peel? I am too much of a Gemini South Node to want to spend time peeling carrots. Pesticides are not just in the skin, they are in the whole carrot. If the carrot isn't organic, peeling doesn't work for health reasons. Most people do it for the aesthetics – a peeled carrot looks better. However, if you are tossing them into a pot roast or going to grind them into a soup, just scrub them well.

To Their Health

Fish Provencal

Taureans like good food but good food is not always good for them. Being stubborn to the core, they will insist on continuing to eat their rich, high calorie foods. However, this dish is so rich with veggies and wine and garlic they will forget that it is good for them too.

2 tablespoons extra-virgin olive oil, divided
1 medium white onion, diced
5 garlic cloves, diced
   (you can add up to 8 cloves depending
   on how much zing you want in the dish)
1 ½ cups mushrooms, sliced
10 medium juicy tomatoes, diced
1 teaspoon kosher salt
4 8-ounce fillets of fish
   Snapper or cod will work; for a milder taste you can use rockfish.
   This really works with any white fish you like and I have had success even with salmon.

3 tablespoons fresh flat-leaf Italian parsley, diced
½ teaspoon freshly ground black pepper
1 teaspoon fresh oregano, minced
1 teaspoon fresh thyme, minced
¼ cup white wine
½ cup pitted Kalamata olives
3 teaspoons capers

Serves 4

Preheat the oven to 375 degrees.

Heat 1 tablespoon of the oil in a large sauté pan over medium-low heat; add the onion and cook about 8 minutes until soft and begins to brown. Add the garlic and cook for 2 minutes – don't burn. Add the mushrooms and cook until soft– about 2–4 minutes. Add the tomatoes, salt, pepper, herbs and wine and cook until soft – about 15 minutes. Stir occasionally to keep the food from sticking and to be sure the veggies are incorporated. Add the olives and capers and cook another 5 minutes. The wine should be reduced by half.

Place the other tablespoon of olive oil in a baking pan. Add the fish fillets turning them once to coat them in oil. Bake for 5 minutes, remove from the oven and then heap the vegetable mixture on top of the fish fillets. Cover loosely with aluminum foil. Place in the oven and cook for 15–20 minutes until the fish is opaque.

Sprinkle the parsley over top and serve immediately.

A note on the battle of the parsleys: Yes, the flat-leaf Italian parsley has better taste than the curly stuff. Try a taste test yourself. The curly stuff is more popular because it is a cheap way to decorate a plate but it tastes not much better than the plate!

Opposites Attract: Stretching your Taurus South Node

The move from Taurus to Scorpio is all about going from Earth-based – what can be touched, smelled, quantified in a very physical sense to a mystical internal journey. Taurus says "I feel;" Scorpio says "I sense." Taurus is Earth; Scorpio is about a watery exploration of the spiritual mystery.

To move your bull along a more spiritual path, make them some of these cookies served on ice cream and drizzled with more chocolate sauce. When they are melting into Taurus heaven, say, "You know, chocolate was a mystical drink to the Aztecs" and see where the conversation takes you! Of course, if your Taurus has done a lot of progressing into Scorpio they will know a lot about Aztec chocolate rituals so you had better be prepared for a lecture on the subject.

Chocolate Cloud Cookies with Vanilla Ice Cream and Chocolate Sauce

Note – this dough needs to sit overnight so plan accordingly.

4 tablespoons unsalted butter
20 ounces of dark chocolate, roughly chopped and divided
½ cup granulated brown sugar
2 large eggs
2 teaspoons pure vanilla extract

1 ½ cups all-purpose flour
¼ teaspoon kosher salt
½ teaspoon baking powder
1 quart vanilla ice cream

Makes about 25

Fill the bottom of a double boiler with water. In the top, melt 8 ounces of the chocolate with the butter over medium-low heat. (You can improvise with a pan and a stainless steel bowl on top but be careful.) Remove from the heat and let it cool but not harden.

While the chocolate is melting, beat the eggs and sugar with an electric beater until thick, pale and fluffy. (You will know it is done when you slowly raise the beaters and the batter falls back into the bowl in slow ribbons.) Gently stir in the vanilla and the chocolate.

In a separate bowl whisk together the flour, salt and baking powder. Add dry ingredients to the chocolate mixture. Don't over stir this – just make sure everything is incorporated together. Cover with plastic wrap and refrigerate until firm; overnight is best.

Preheat the oven to 325 degrees and place the rack in the center of oven.

Line cookie sheets with parchment paper. Form the dough into 1 inch balls and place on the sheets about an inch and half apart. Work quickly as you don't want them to get too hot.

Bake the cookies 10-13 minutes or just until the edges are slightly firm but the centers still soft. Remove from the oven and place on a wire rack to cool.

In the double boiler melt the remaining chocolate over medium-low heat. Once it is melted, lower the heat and just keep the chocolate warm.

When the cookies are cool, serve them over a scoop of good vanilla ice cream and drizzle the warm chocolate sauce over them.

Dessert

Basil Pesto and Cheese Torte

I first had this dish at a potluck. I had never seen one of these as a dessert. It was interesting but had an odd tang. I played with it for a bit and came up with this torte which is easy to make and very pretty.

> 30 ounces mascarpone cheese, softened
> 10 ounces goat cheese, softened
> 1 cup basil pesto (See pesto recipe on page 25 and substitute basil for mint)
>
> Serves 8 – 10

Beat the cheeses together in a large mixing bowl. Layer an 8 inch springform pan with ½ of the cheese mixture. Layer half the pesto on top and then the rest of the cheese. Spread the remaining pesto on the top. Refrigerate 4 hours or overnight.

Just before serving pop the springform pan and serve. Cut in thin slices as this is rich even for Taurus.

If you don't have a springform pan or prefer to make this dish in cute little ramekins go ahead. I think people prefer having their own little dessert anyway and it will appeal to the hoarder aspect of Taurus.

Famous People with
Taurus South Node –
Scorpio North Node

Sharon Stone –

In her heyday, her body and several strategic parts of it were her thing. She was all about her physicality. Even going to the Academy Awards, wearing a simple man-tailored shirt, brought attention to her body. At her wedding to Phil Bronstein, she served caviar, *foie gras* and veal chops – all rich Taurus foods.

Kate Winslet –

She is someone with a very Taurus body who proudly showed off her curves and told Hollywood that this is what a real woman should look like. In 2008 she was quoted in *Parade Magazine* as saying, "We were having lunch, and I was having a glass of wine and eating bread and putting butter on the bread, and I turned to Sam and said, 'I am just so happy!'" She went on to say there is nothing like butter. Creamy, creamy butter is tough for the tactile Taurus to forsake.

Taurus North Node Honoré de Balzac was known for his gluttonous binges. In *La Comedie Humaine* he listed over 15 different fish dishes. It is reported that he once binged on nothing but onions. I did say that Taurus tends to horde didn't I?

gemini
Chapter 5

Faster than a speeding bullet, grabbing information seemingly out of thin air, Gemini is all about speed and knowledge. The archetype of Gemini is the little yellow guy on the FTD flower trucks, speeding along to his destination. Actually that little yellow man is a take on the ancient symbol for the god Mercury. (I love when modern businesses invoke the ancient gods but yet so many think Astrology is a silly thing.) Mercury is our fastest planet, zipping around the Sun in only 88 days. Someone deeply into the sign of Gemini doesn't have the patience to sit around for complicated dinners.

The 3rd house is the where Gemini is most secure; the house of communication, education and relating that information to our peers. Gemini is symbolized by the twins, the sign of duality and it is not uncommon for a Gemini to argue one issue and then take the opposite view with the same vehemence. It is all about getting out the information – any information – for them.

Positive aspects of Gemini include:
versatility, good communication skills and the love of information, education and conversation.

Shadow aspects of Gemini include:
nervousness, irresponsibility, inconsistency, and the inability to commit to pretty much anything of permanence.

Foodie aspects of Gemini include:
a love of dual tastes which appeals to their twin nature, fast foods and foods that encourage movement and conversation.

Famous People with Gemini Rising

Tony Blair – Known for his ability to communicate well to his people. Do you remember the "People's Princess" speech he made after the death of Princess Diana? In such a typical Gemini fashion, when he was asked about his favorite food he said spaghetti, another time he said fish and chips and then he made a local London haddock shop famous because he went there so often and said that theirs was his favorite.

Kathie Lee Gifford – Well, as I said, the shadow is irresponsibility. She is a great example of the Gemini who keeps chattering on. Remember when she gushed over Martin Short about his wife and their terrific marriage – even though his wife happened to be dead for a more than a year? Anyway, I found one of her favorite recipes on an NBC website called "Tasty Morsels." How Gemini is that – only time for a morsel?

Appetizer

Geminis like to talk and eat. Well, they like to talk and do just about everything. This is a good "grab and go" appetizer that is good for a crowd. Gemini loves to hold forth in front of a crowd. This does require some marinating time so plan accordingly.

Chicken Lollipops

2 pounds chicken wings
2 tablespoons soy sauce
8 garlic cloves, roughly chopped
2 adobo chilies, roughly chopped
1 teaspoon white wine vinegar
1 tablespoon fresh ginger, thinly sliced

1 tablespoon paprika
1 teaspoon kosher salt
3 eggs, beaten
1 ½ cups panko bread crumbs
2 cups canola oil

Serves 8

Slice through the joints of the chicken wings and cut off the tips. Grab the part of the wing that has the single bone and gently push the meat towards the end of the bone. Use a paring knife to scrape the meat off of the bone so that you have a clean bone "handle" and all of the meat on one end of the wing. Take the part of the wing with the 2 bones and start scraping the meat toward one end. Remove the smaller of the 2 bones and again, clean the bone while pushing the meat to the end. Folks, this sounds spookier than it is, trust me. Aries and Sagittarius don't get crazy with the knife, and Pisces and Aquarius don't go off into la-la land and you will be fine.

In a large bowl mix the soy sauce, garlic, chilies, vinegar, ginger, paprika and salt. Place the chicken wings in the sauce, cover and refrigerate for 1–4 hours.

Whisk the eggs in a large bowl and spread the panko on a sheet of wax paper.

Heat the oil in an electric frying pan or Dutch oven over medium-low heat. Dip the meat part of each chicken wing in the egg and then roll in the panko. Gently place in the oil and cook for about 8–10 minutes until the bread crumbs start to turn medium brown. Drain the cooked chicken on a large dish covered with paper towels. Serve immediately.

A note on frying: To test that your oil is hot enough sprinkle a few breadcrumbs over it. If they start to bubble it is ready, if they sit there like a dead fish, it isn't hot enough and if they explode lower the heat for goodness sake!

Soup

Jean Garofalo Porte's Escarole, Sausage and Bean Soup

I love soup but I also have that Gemini South Node which makes me impatient, especially when I am dying for a good bowl of soup. As usual Mom came to the rescue. This is my mother's delicious escarole, sausage and bean soup that is fast and yummy. I often use kale in place of the escarole which is hard to find in some areas. You can really use any hearty green; collards work fine too. This soup freezes very well so you can make some batches up and defrost quickly when Gemini drops by with his latest book club or two.

2 tablespoons extra-virgin olive oil
4 garlic cloves, minced
1 ½ pounds good Italian sausage
   – mild or spicy depending on your preference
1 teaspoon fresh thyme, minced
1 15-ounce can cannellini (white kidney) beans

4 cups chicken stock
   (you can use canned but for more taste
   make your own – see page 44)
2 heads escarole, washed and roughly chopped*
1 cup Parmigiano-Reggiano cheese, shaved

Serves 6

In a large soup pot heat the oil over medium heat, add the garlic and sauté carefully until lightly browned. Garlic burns fast so be careful. Remove the garlic to a side dish. Add the sausage and cook on each side about 3 minutes, until it is well browned. Stir in the thyme. Remove the sausage, let cool and cut into ¼-inch pieces. Return the sausage pieces to the soup pot add the beans and stir to combine totally. Pour in the chicken stock and bring to boil. Add the escarole and cook about 3 minutes.

Place in bowls and shave the cheese over the top before serving.

*Whatever green you use needs to be small enough to fit on a spoon. You don't want your guests having to cut the greens in their soup.

A note on garlic peeling: One trick to get that pesky peel off of garlic is to cut off the root part and then smash the remaining head with the heel of your hand against a cutting board or counter. Place the head in a bowl and cover it with another bowl of the same size. Shake it like a crazy person for a few minutes. When you take the top bowl off you should see that the peel is off.

Pasta

Pasta e Fagiole, What We Called "Pasta Fazool"

We are playing a little trick here because in his Greek incarnation, Mercury, Gemini's ruler, was called Hermes and was considered the trickster. This is actually a soup but it has pasta in it so I am making it a "pasta."

2 tablespoons extra-virgin olive oil

4 ounces pancetta, diced

1 cup white onions, chopped

3 celery stalks, diced

3 large carrots, diced

3 garlic cloves, minced

2 tablespoons fresh thyme, minced

2 tablespoons fresh flat-leaf Italian parsley, minced

1 15-ounce can red kidney beans, drained and rinsed

16 ounces fresh tomato sauce (see page 24) or a 16-ounce can of plum tomatoes that have been run through your food processor for about 45 seconds.

4 cups chicken stock (see page 44 if you want to make your own)

¾ cup ditali macaroni*

2 teaspoons kosher salt

1 teaspoon freshly ground black pepper

⅓ cup Parmigiano-Reggiano cheese, grated

Serves 6

Heat the oil in a medium soup pan over medium heat. Add the pancetta and cook for about 8 minutes until lightly browned. Remove the pancetta to a small dish to cool and add the onions, celery and carrots to the pan. Sauté about 10 minutes until lightly browned. Add the garlic, sauté for another 2 minutes and then stir in the herbs and cook 1 minute. Stir in the beans, tomato sauce and chicken stock. Bring to a low boil stirring occasionally. Add the macaroni, salt and pepper. Cook about 10 minutes, until the macaroni is *al dente*. Stir often because the macaroni sticks. Sprinkle cheese on top and serve immediately.

*Small pasta is small pasta. Mom used ditali but if you are into orzo go with it. Any small pasta will do.

Veggies & Fruit

Cold Broccoli and Olive Salad

We used to have this on Christmas Eve when I was a kid. It has a wonderful taste and is made quickly – you know how that appeals to Mr. Mercury.

2 large heads fresh broccoli florets, trimmed and washed
1 medium white onion, diced
1 7.5-ounce can black olives
3 tablespoons red wine vinegar
3 tablespoons extra-virgin olive oil
2 teaspoons kosher salt
2 teaspoons freshly ground black pepper
1 teaspoon fresh thyme, minced
2 garlic cloves, minced

Serves 6 – 8

Heat 1–2 quarts of water in a medium sauce pan over medium-high heat. Add the broccoli and cook until just soft – about 5 minutes. Drain and rinse in cold water to stop the cooking process. Drain again and transfer to a medium bowl and allow the broccoli to get cold.

Add the rest of the ingredients to the broccoli and mix really well. Cover and refrigerate for 2–4 hours before serving.

Baked Stuffed Onions

These take a while in the oven but the preparation time is quick. Gemini can throw the onions in the oven and then go read a book or two, or three......

5 tablespoons extra-virgin olive oil
1 teaspoon each kosher salt and freshly ground black pepper
4 red onions, peeled and sliced in half horizontally
6 ounces goat cheese (you can use feta if you don't like goat, I have used Gouda and it was fine)
1 egg yolk
2 tablespoons fresh basil leaves, diced
2 tablespoons fresh oregano, diced

Serves 4

Preheat the oven to 300 degrees.

Mix the salt and pepper with the olive oil and brush lightly over the sliced onions. Place on a baking sheet and bake for about an hour, until soft.

In a small bowl mix the rest of the ingredients until fully combined. Store in the refrigerator until the onions are ready. This can be made up to 4 hours ahead.

When the onions are cooked remove from the oven and cool. Scoop out the heart of the onion carefully. You don't want to break the walls of the onion.

Put the onion hearts in a food processor and pulverize. Add the cheese mixture, combining well. Fill each onion with the cheese mixture. Place under a low heat broiler for about 30 seconds – just until the cheese begins to bubble. Serve immediately

A note on fresh herbs: If you have a window somewhere in your house you can have fresh herbs all year round. They don't take a lot of room – a simple, small flower pot works. If you have a patio you can place them out there in the summer and bring them in for the winter. It is worth it, there is nothing like fresh picked herbs in your food.

Meat & Fish

Steak and Tuna Medallions

Although Gemini is not the only sign of duality (Pisces is symbolized by two fish going in opposite directions), it is known as the sign of the twins. So I will honor Gemini with this tasty offering – a fun take on twin medallions.

1 cup extra-virgin olive oil, divided

1 cup orange juice, divided

3 teaspoons kosher salt, divided

4 teaspoons freshly ground black pepper, divided

1 teaspoon fresh oregano, minced

1 teaspoon fresh thyme, minced

4 5–6-ounce pieces tuna – best to get sushi grade; if you can get them cut into blocks they will look more like steak

Serves 4

4 5–6-ounce beef fillet medallions

3 garlic cloves, minced

½ cup flat-leaf Italian parsley, chopped, divided

½ cup white wine

4 teaspoons grated orange zest

♈ ♉ ♊ ♋ ♌ ♍ ♎ ♏ ♐ ♑ ♒ ♓

In a medium bowl combine the oil, ½ cup of the juice, 1 teaspoon of the salt, 2 teaspoons of the pepper, oregano and thyme. Add the tuna, turn to coat with the oil mixture, cover and refrigerate and let marinate for about an hour.

Generously salt and pepper the beef medallions. Combine the garlic, all but 1 teaspoon of the parsley, wine, and olive oil in small bowl and stir. Brush this mixture on both sides of the beef medallions.

If you are using a charcoal grill build a medium flame and then cook the beef medallions about 5 minutes on each side to get good grill marks; continue cooking and turning until the center registers 135 degrees on a meat thermometer.

About 5 minutes before the steak is done, put the tuna on the grill and sear 3 minutes on each side. Remove the meat and tuna from the grill and let the beef rest for 5 minutes before cutting.

You can also heat 3 tablespoons of olive oil in large skillet or electric frying pan and then cook the tuna and beef.

Boil the rest of the orange juice in a medium saucepan for about 2 minutes (or the skillet you cooked the meat and fish in if you did that.) Remove from the heat. Arrange the tuna and beef in a dish and pour the orange juice over them and sprinkle with the orange zest and remaining parsley. Serve immediately.

A note on grills: Gas Grills, really folks? The whole purpose of grilling is to get the charcoal taste. Now I know there are some health issues surrounding the use of charcoal but summer is short – enjoy the charcoal while you can. (If you live where summer is not short – then use some discretion.) You might as well just cook on a gas stove instead of hassling with a gas grill. Gas grills don't impart any more flavor than a gas stove.

Bison, Pork, Sausage Chili

I used this recipe to win a chili cook-off at an office where I do some volunteer work. (I also won another time with my stuffed pumpkin that is elsewhere in this book.) This one has a kick to it – so play with the peppers to see how much heat you like. For a more intense flavor use dark beer and beef stock instead of chicken.

2 pounds pork loin, diced
2 pounds ground bison meat
1 pound sausage – hot or mild depending on taste, diced
2–3 tablespoons freshly ground black pepper
2 tablespoons kosher salt
1 ½ teaspoons ground cinnamon, divided
3 teaspoons ground cumin, divided
4 tablespoons chili powder, divided
¼ – ½ cup corn meal
¼ cup extra-virgin olive oil
4 medium white onions, peeled, diced

1 medium green pepper, seeded and diced
6 garlic cloves, minced
2 jalapeno peppers, sliced thinly with seeds, stems removed
1 small can chipotle peppers in adobo sauce
2 cups crushed tomatoes
¼ cup honey
2 teaspoons dried oregano
2–3 (12-ounce) bottles beer
1 quart chicken stock (for homemade see page 44)
12 ounces of pinto beans, which have been soaked overnight
2–4 ounces semisweet chocolate, cut into large chunks

Serves 10 – 15

Place the meat in a large bowl. Season it with the salt and pepper, ½ teaspoon of the cinnamon, 1 teaspoon of the cumin, and 2 tablespoons of the chili powder, then coat the meat with the corn meal. Make sure the meat is well coated with the seasonings and corn meal.

Preheat a cast iron Dutch oven on the stove over medium-high heat. Add the olive oil and then the coated meat. Make just 1 layer of meat on the bottom of the oven, don't bunch it up. You will have to do this in batches. Don't turn the meat a lot, let it brown and caramelize well. Once all sides are caramelized, remove the meat from the pan with a slotted spoon to a platter to cool.

Add the onions, green pepper and garlic to the Dutch oven and sauté for 5 minutes over medium heat until they start to caramelize and get soft. Add the jalapenos and allow to cook for 2 more minutes until soft. Add the chipotle peppers and sauce and the remaining 2 teaspoons of the cumin, 1 teaspoon of the cinnamon, the oregano, and 2 heaping tablespoons of the chili powder. Add tomatoes, honey, oregano and beer. Stir to incorporate everything very well. Return the reserved meat to the Dutch oven. Add chicken stock and beans. Simmer over low heat for 1½–2 hours until the meat is tender. (You can also place the pan in the oven and cook at 350 degrees for the same amount of time.) Check to be sure the chili hasn't dried out – add more stock if necessary.

Stir in the chocolate and simmer another 1–2 hours. Again, make sure it doesn't dry out or burn. I don't like watery chili – I like it thicker but again that is a personal taste.

Serve with the cumin infused sour cream and corny cord bread (see recipes page 73.)

Cumin Infused Sour Cream

In a small sauté pan toast 3 tablespoons of cumin over low heat for about 2 minutes.
Stir into 12 ounces of sour cream and spoon on top of chili.

Corny Corn Bread

3 tablespoons extra-virgin olive oil
½ cup onions, chopped
¾ cup corn, if fresh, cook it first
   but you can also use canned
1 cup self-rising cornmeal
½ teaspoon baking soda

Serves 6 – 8

¼ teaspoon kosher salt
1 ½ cups cheddar cheese, shredded
½ cup plain yogurt
1 cup milk
2 eggs, beaten

Preheat the oven to 350 degrees.

Heat the oil in a small sauté pan over medium heat and cook the onions until soft and browned, add the corn and stir together for 2 minutes. Combine the ingredients in a large bowl and stir until moistened. Spoon the mixture into a greased 10-inch cast iron skillet or a greased baking dish if you don't have cast iron skillets. Bake for 45 minutes or until browned on top. Let cool on a rack for 30 minutes before serving.

To Their Health

Blueberry Polenta

Geminis have to learn to be relaxed and the area Gemini controls is around the lungs. Berries are good foods for both calming and the pulmonary system so for my Gemini pals I give you something that sounded so odd to me that it appealed to my Gemini curiosity and turned out to be very tasty.

For years we could never figure out why my Aunt Mary De Flora's polenta and gnocchi were so much better than everyone else's. One day she gave me the secret....farina! A bit of farina makes the polenta so light and fluffy! If you live in an area where farina is hard to get use Cream of Rice, it works almost as well.

You can do this for breakfast or a Sunday evening winter meal. I actually prefer it for dinner.

2 teaspoons kosher salt, divided
2 tablespoons butter
1 cup milk
2 teaspoons freshly ground black pepper
1 cup stone-ground yellow corn meal
¼ cup farina
6 ounces mascarpone
   (or cream cheese if you can't get it)

Serves 6

Blueberry sauce

2 cups fresh or frozen blueberries
3 tablespoons honey or agave
Juice of 1 lemon
1 teaspoon lemon zest

A note on berries: Berries – all of them – blue, black, rasp, and straw – freeze wonderfully. Snatch them up fresh in summer; give them a quick wash and drain and freeze in plastic bags. There is nothing like a good berry in February.

For the polenta, boil 5 cups of water with 1 teaspoon of the salt in a medium sauce pan over medium heat. Stir in the butter, milk and the rest of the salt and pepper. Whisk in the corn meal in a slow stream and continue to whisk until there are no lumps. Then whisk in the farina. Lower the heat and simmer for 30 minutes, stirring often. Add more milk if the polenta is drying out. Add the mascarpone and stir.

While the polenta is cooking, place the ingredients for the blueberry sauce mixture in a medium saucepan over low heat for 4 minutes, until soft but not mushy.

Scoop the polenta into bowls and top with the blueberry sauce.

Opposites Attract: Stretching Your Gemini South Node

A Gemini South Node person, like yours truly, is moving into the truth-seeking sign of Sagittarius, who is all about searching the world, interacting with all people on a deeper level and finding out what they believe in. It is a perfect example of "from many – one." From many ways of learning we come into ourselves.

I am choosing this recipe for Moorish Pork Kebobs to help the Gemini move northward because the idea will appeal to their need to converse and mingle and because the Moorish influence will spark their intellectual curiosity. Of course you will have to be prepared for them to start quoting from "Othello." However, because the kebobs are from another country it will help to pull them out of their comfort zone and into the bigger world.

I wish I knew where I got this recipe I just remember that I liked the idea of making something that was a bit exotic so it wound up in my collection (Gemini South Node – remember?)

Moorish Pork Kebobs

For the best flavor, this meat should be refrigerated overnight. If you don't have that long, marinate it for at least four hours.

6 tablespoons extra-virgin olive oil, divided
4 tablespoons ground cumin
2 tablespoons ground paprika
2 teaspoons cayenne pepper
2 teaspoons fresh oregano, minced
2 teaspoons fresh thyme, minced
1 teaspoon kosher salt
1 teaspoon freshly ground black pepper
½ teaspoon fresh ginger, diced
4 garlic cloves, minced

½ cup flat-leaf Italian parsley, minced
¼ cup fresh lemon juice
2 pounds pork loin, cubed
Wooden or steel meat skewers
1 each red, yellow and green pepper, cubed
1 white onion, cubed

Serves 8

Heat 4 tablespoons of the oil in a small sauté pan over low heat and add all of the spices from the cumin to black pepper and warm them slowly – about 3 minutes. This really brings out the fragrance and taste of the herbs. Set them aside to cool.

In a medium bowl place the ginger, garlic, parsley, lemon juice and the cooled herbs. Mix very well then add the meat and turn until all the meat is covered. Cover with plastic wrap and refrigerate overnight.

If using wooden skewers, place them in a large bowl of water for about 4 hours before cooking.

Thread the meat, peppers and onion on to the wooden skewers. If using a grill, cook over a low flame about 5 minutes on each side. You can also broil under a low flame in the oven.

Serve immediately – it goes great with basmati rice!

A note on skewers: If you make kebobs a lot, invest in a set of steel skewers. Just be careful when you take them off the grill – use your mitts because they get hot.

♈ ♉ ♊ ♋ ♌ ♍ ♎ ♏ ♐ ♑ ♒ ♓

Raspberry and Blueberry Lemon Mini-Tarts

This will appeal to the Gemini's love for variety. They do hate to be bored! If you have the need to make your own tart shells go ahead. There are many recipes out there or just ask the neighborhood Cancer, they have all such recipes. Sorry, but baking bores me! I am still too much of an impatient Gemini to love the precision required in baking so I buy mini-tarts. You can even buy really good British lemon curd although it is easy and fun to make.

The great thing is you can make the curd and toppings and even the tarts in advance, freeze them and put them together quickly for a great dessert.

For Lemon Curd	Raspberry Topping	Blueberry Topping
Zest of 3 lemons	1 ½ cups fresh raspberries	1 ½ cups fresh blueberries
1 cup sugar	2 tablespoons minced lemon zest	2 tablespoons fresh lemon juice
¼ pound unsalted butter		
5 egg yolks		
Juice of 4 lemons		

Makes about 20 tarts.

Put the lemon zest in a food processor. Pulse in the sugar until it is all minced together.

Cream the butter in a large mixing bowl. Mix in the lemon mixture. When the butter and lemon are combined well, beat in the egg yolks, one at a time. When well blended, mix in the lemon juice.

Cook the lemon mixture in a medium saucepan over low heat while stirring constantly until it begins to thicken, 10–15 minutes. Take off the heat and refrigerate until cool.

For the other toppings mix the berries and lemon in two separate bowls until well blended.

When the curd is cool, fill the tarts with the curd and then alternate between the raspberry and blueberry toppings. Serve immediately.

Dessert

Famous People
with
Gemini South Node –
Sagittarius North Node

William Shakespeare –

Here is a great example of someone who obviously used his past Gemini lives to gather the knowledge that he needed to write those brilliant works of art. In his Shakespeare incarnation he was able to settle far enough into his Sagittarian North Node to sit down and write out what he had gathered over time. Admittedly we don't really know what kind of food he liked, but I found a very Gemini-esque line in "Henry V", "I would give all my fame for a pot of ale." Sure because a Gemini can drink ale on the run; – a Taurus would have said "for rich cake."

Nelson Mandela –

He is clearly someone who is exhibiting a great progression into his North Node. He used his Gemini ability to keep communicating under the harshest of conditions but was able to express true compassion even for his captors – a very expansive Jupiter thing to do! (Jupiter rules Sagittarius) His favorite food is more Sagittarius than Gemini too. It is oxtail stew, something that is long- cooking and can be savored while reading a good, deep book.

Gemini North Node Freddie Mercury's favorite
foods were chili and ribs – always on the
move those Geminis.

cancer
Chapter 6

Cancer or "Moon Child", its politically correct name these days is all about – hello – the Moon, which is our emotional barometer. The 4th house, the natural home for Moon Child, is the home of our roots, our family, and our mother. Cancer is symbolized by the crab. When they are hurt crabs will retreat into their shells. It is almost impossible to coax grumpy crabs from their shells but, still pouting a bit, they will eventually emerge, especially if they can be coaxed by some good comfort food.

Positive aspects of Cancer include:
patriotism, being family-oriented and having leadership –
executive abilities and a deep compassion for those who are in need.

The shadow aspects of Cancer include:
moodiness, hyper-emotionalism, shutting down emotionally to others, and being a "smother-mother."

Foodie aspects of Cancer include:
home-spun foods, foods gentle to the stomach and food with a nod to the historical.

Famous People with Cancer Rising

Cass Elliott – Of course we called her "Momma Cass." Cancer is the momma of the Zodiac. She did NOT die by choking on a ham sandwich, as was erroneously reported. However, she obviously had her issues with fattening, comfort foods.

Judy Garland – Another songbird who had food issues, although hers were caused by stupid studio bosses with bizarre ideas on how a woman's body should be shaped. It is said that her favorite food was steak and kidney pie. While not a staple for most Americans, it is a quintessential British comfort food made by many a British mum. Ironically, she would die in England.

♈ ♉ ♊ ♋ ♌ ♍ ♎ ♏ ♐ ♑ ♒ ♓

Macaroni Pie

This was normally served as an Italian dessert at Easter-time when I was a kid but you can also cut the pie into little squares and serve as an appetizer. It provides the comfort of carbs and Cancerians love recipes handed down from a previous generation.

    3 teaspoons kosher salt, divided
    ½ pound elbow macaroni
    7 large eggs, beaten
    3 pounds ricotta cheese
    ½ cup Parmigiano-Reggiano cheese, grated
    1 teaspoon freshly ground black pepper

    Makes about 50 1-inch by 1-inch squares.

Preheat the oven to 400 degrees.

Cook the macaroni in 4 quarts of water and 2 teaspoons of the salt until *al dente* – about 8–10 minutes.

While the pasta is cooking, mix all of the ingredients in a large bowl until thoroughly combined. When the pasta is cooked, drain and allow to cool for a minute. Mix it into the cheese mixture stirring constantly to be sure that the eggs don't start to scramble.

Pour the ingredients into a well-greased 3-quart baking pan.

Bake for 15 minutes and then reduce the heat to 325 degrees. Cook another 45–60 minutes, until the top is lightly browned and an inserted toothpick comes out dry. Cool on a wire rack, cut into squares and refrigerate. Macaroni pie can be served cold or at room temperature.

This can be stored in the refrigerator for 2–3 days.

Appetizer

Soup

Stracciatella -Italian Egg Drop Soup

Growing up I didn't know this soup had a fancy Italian name. We always called it "Mom's Italian Egg Drop Soup." She always made it on New Year's Day when we were all tired of heavy holiday fare. Shortly before she died I showed Mom a similar recipe in the *New York Times* food section, although the author used a heavier, grainier cracker. She shook her head – nope, hers was better than the *New York Times*. Having tried both I realized she was right. This is the Italian version of Jewish chicken soup and can make even a moody Cancer smile.

> 3 quarts chicken stock (see page 44 for my homemade stock)
>   – you can use good vegetable stock if you prefer a vegetarian variety
> 1 10-ounce box of crackers such Krispy or Zesta*
> 10 medium eggs
> 2 teaspoons freshly ground black pepper
> ½ cup Parmigiano-Reggiano cheese, grated
> ¼ cup flat-leaf Italian parsley, finely chopped
>
> Serves 6

Bring the chicken stock to a gentle rolling boil in a large soup pot over medium heat. While the stock is heating, crush the crackers into small crumbs. (Mom used to do this with a rolling pin, having placed the crackers between 2 pieces of wax paper. I use the food processor. The Cancerians and Capricorns may feel nostalgic to use the good old-fashioned rolling pin. Gemini South Node here likes the fast processor!)

Beat the eggs in a large bowl, and then add the pepper, parsley and cracker crumbs. Mix well.

When the stock is gently boiling, slowly pour the egg mixture in a fine stream mixing as you pour to prevent the eggs from scrambling. Continue to stir the soup until it comes to a gentle boil again. Check for salt – you might have to add a bit depending on the type of cracker you use. Serve immediately.

*When my mother started to make this in the 1930s Uneeda Biscuits were on the market. Sadly they are no more. Krispy or Zesta can work but watch the salt. If the crackers have salt, don't add any to the soup. If they are unsalted, add 2 teaspoons kosher salt when you add the pepper.

Pasta

Comfort Polenta

People with a lot of Moon Child in their charts often have weak stomachs so spicy pastas don't always agree with their constitutions. This recipe was inspired by watching my Aunt Mary Garofalo De Flora make her polenta. I have added some mascarpone cheese to modernize it and a bit of sage for zing. It is a perfect winter comfort food dish that evokes memories of the comforts of childhood.

I know I used blueberry polenta before but this is a different beast and shows how versatile a little corn meal can be.

> 1 tablespoon extra-virgin olive oil
> 5 sage leaves
> 1 teaspoon kosher salt
> 3 cups yellow cornmeal
> 1 cup farina (or cream of rice if you can't find farina)
> 1 ½ cups Parmigiano-Reggiano cheese, grated
> 1 cup mascarpone cheese
> ½ teaspoon freshly ground black pepper
> 2 ½ cups milk, room temperature
> ½ cup unsalted butter
>
> Serves 10 – 12

Heat the oil in a small saucepan over low heat then slowly sauté the sage leaves for about 10 seconds. Immediately remove to a plate covered with a paper towel.

Bring 3 quarts of water and the salt to a boil in a large saucepan over high heat. Reduce the heat to low and slowly whisk in the cornmeal and then the farina. Continue to stir and cook until the mixture thickens – about 20 minutes. Remove the pot from the heat. Stir in the cheeses, pepper, milk and butter, and continue stirring until the cheese is melted and fully incorporated.

Crumble the sage leaves over the top of each dish and serve immediately.

Veggies & Fruit

Rose Weinstock's Mock Chopped Liver

My friend Arlene Weinstock claims that her mother made the best mock chopped liver. Arlene is one of those Virgo vegetarian types so I humored her, but after tasting it I have to agree! You can engage your Cancer in a discussion of Jewish cookery in America while preparing this; you know how they are about tradition.

1 tablespoon extra-virgin olive oil
1 large white onion, chopped
2 medium eggs, hard boiled and shelled
1 pound green beans, trimmed
¼ to ⅓ cup walnuts (adjust thickness with
    more or fewer nuts)*

Serves 4 – 6

2 garlic cloves, diced
1 teaspoon kosher salt
1 teaspoon freshly ground black pepper

In a medium sauté pan over medium heat warm the oil. Reduce the heat, add the onions and caramelize until dark brown – about 15–30 minutes. In a medium stock pot over medium heat add the green beans and about 1 cup of water. The beans should be half covered. Blanch the beans until they just begin to get soft – about 3 minutes.

Put all of the ingredients into a food processor in small batches and process until very soft and pliable. Put the batches into a large bowl and mix. Adjust seasoning – check salt and pepper. Place in a mold or just a pretty serving dish. Serve lightly chilled or at room temperature. I like to serve it with celery sticks, cucumber slices, carrot slices or crackers.

*If nuts do evil things to you as they do me – use peanuts, or pine nuts. Heck, raisins will do in a pinch.

A note on caramelizing onions: I have followed recipes that say you can caramelize onions in 15- 20 minutes but I have found that not to be true. Frankly, you can cook them low and slow for up to an hour or more. The longer they cook, the yummier they get. Just keep the heat low so they don't burn.

Stuffed Pumpkin

This is one of my favorite Thanksgiving recipes that doubles as a great centerpiece. It pretty much screams "home and hearth and I am all about tradition, holidays and a warm and comfortable home." You can also do individual sugar pumpkins and serve one per person, which is always a cute addition to the fall table.

1 5–7-pound pumpkin or 6–8 small sugar pumpkins
8 pieces bacon
1 cup white onions, diced
1 cup shitake mushrooms, sliced
2 tablespoons kosher salt
3 tablespoons freshly ground black pepper
4 garlic cloves, sliced

Serves 6 – 8

1 tablespoon fresh thyme, minced
1 pound bread, cubed – any kind of bread works depending on your taste
1 ½ pounds Gruyere, Fontina or Emmenthaler cheese, cubed
1 cup heavy cream
½ teaspoon freshly grated nutmeg

Preheat the oven to 350 degrees.

Cut off the top of the pumpkin and remove the seeds and flesh.*

In a medium saucepan over medium heat, cook the bacon until crisp. Remove to a plate covered with a paper towel.

In the same pan (you may have to pour off excess fat, you don't want more than a couple of tablespoons), sauté the onions about 10-15 minutes; add the mushrooms, salt, pepper and garlic and sauté another 2 minutes. Add the thyme.

In a large bowl, combine the onion mix with the rest of the ingredients and crumble in the bacon. Spoon the mixture into the pumpkin. If it is dry add more cream.

Place the top on the pumpkin and transfer to the oven; cook until the filling is bubbling and the pumpkin flesh is tender – about 2 hours. Place on a large serving platter and serve warm.

*A note on pumpkin seeds: Place the seeds in a greased cookie sheet, sprinkle with salt and cayenne pepper and bake for about 20 minutes in a 250-degree oven or until the seeds are nicely browned.

Meat & Fish

Mom's Meatloaf

I know, I know. What is the big deal about meatloaf? Everyone has a meatloaf recipe. Yes, but this one is different and extra homey. I have always found meatloaf to be a good meal when my stomach is just coming back from a bad spell, which happens often to our Cancerian friends. All of that emotion is tough on their digestion. Serve it family style with some creamy mashed potatoes and they will be your buddies for life.

4 medium eggs, hard boiled and shelled
1 tablespoon extra-virgin olive oil
3 cups onions, chopped
2 garlic cloves, finely chopped
1 teaspoon fresh thyme, minced
2 teaspoons fresh flat-leaf Italian parsley, minced
2 teaspoons kosher salt
1 teaspoon freshly ground black pepper
¼ cup Dijon mustard – not the yellow hot dog stuff

Serves 6

3 tablespoons Worcestershire sauce
1 pound lean, ground beef
1 ½ pounds ground pork
½ cup plain bread crumbs
2 large eggs, beaten
1 cup tomato sauce – you can cheat and buy canned stuffed – or use the recipe for Mom's "gravy" on page 24

A note on mustard: I try to stay away from the yellow stuff. Dijon is my favorite, although I am not a fan of the gritty ones that have a lot of seed left. Play around with mustards – I have found Trader Joe's Dijon to be my favorite.

Preheat the oven to 325 degrees.

Heat the oil in a medium sauté pan over medium heat and cook the onions until soft – about 3–5 minutes and slightly brown. Stir in the garlic, thyme, parsley, salt and pepper and heat for a few minutes. Don't let the garlic burn. Remove from heat and cool.

In a large bowl mix together the mustard, Worcestershire sauce, beef, pork, bread crumbs, onion/garlic mixture and beaten eggs. The best way to do this is with your hands but don't overwork. (Give this task to an impatient Air Sign person.) Gently work the meat into a rectangular loaf but leave about ¼ on the side. When the base of the loaf is complete, nestle the hard boiled eggs along the top. Cover the eggs completely with the rest of the meat so they are totally unseen. Leave them whole – just lay them gently on top and then cover.

Place the loaf on a greased 2-quart baking pan. Pour the tomato sauce over the top making sure it coats the loaf. Place this pan inside a large roasting pan and fill the roasting pan ½ way up with water. Bake for about an hour, until the internal temperature is 160 degrees and the meatloaf is cooked through. Serve hot.

The eggs inside are not only a nice surprise but add moistness to the meat loaf.

A note on bread crumbs: My mother always kept pieces of bread that had gone hard in a brown bag in a drawer next to the potatoes. I just remember always seeing the bread and potatoes together. Anyway, when the bag got full she would brown the bread in a 300-degree oven for about 20-30 minutes and then grate the slices into crumbs when they cooled. I do the same thing but cheat and use a food processor instead of grating. It is a great way to "recycle."

Brunswick Stew

Cancerians are the flag-waving patriots of the Zodiac. This dish will appeal to them because it is based on an Early American dish and because stews are homey. I think I got this recipe at some historical home I visited a while ago. Since it started with "two squirrels," I had to do more than a bit of tweaking. Even an adventurous Sagittarius or hearty Capricorn would turn up their noses at squirrel – maybe.

1 2-3-pound chicken
3 tablespoons extra-virgin olive oil
2 large white onions, diced
1 pound pancetta, cubed
4 medium sweet potatoes, cubed
3 garlic cloves, diced
2 pounds beef brisket
4 pounds fresh roasted tomatoes (see page 21) or 1 28-ounce can of crushed tomatoes

1 cup frozen lima beans, or if you hate limas like me, use peas instead
1 16-ounce can corn
2 cups red wine
1 tablespoon Worcestershire sauce
1 teaspoon kosher salt
1 teaspoon freshly ground black pepper

Serves 8

Preheat the oven to 325 degrees.

Place the chicken in a greased roasting pan and bake for an hour. When cooled to the touch, remove the meat from the bones. Discard the skin and bones of the chicken.

In a large Dutch oven heat the oil over medium heat and sauté the onions until they caramelize – about 30 minutes, stirring often. Add the pancetta and potatoes and sauté until lightly browned – about 5–8 minutes; add the garlic and sauté 2 more minutes. Add the beef brisket and sauté about 3 minutes on each side until browned. Stir in the chicken, tomatoes, lima beans, corn, wine, Worchester sauce, salt and pepper.

Place the Dutch oven in the oven and cook for 2–3 hours. Check each hour. If the stew is drying add more wine or some chicken stock. The meat will be very tender and the brisket should come apart easily.

Serve hot.

To Their Health

Icebox "Cake"

Moon Children are consummate worriers – they retreat from the world and worry and brood and then brood and worry and there is always some time left for some more brooding. No one can give the silent treatment better than a Moon Child. What do they need to literally bring them out of their shells and return them to the world? Why chocolate of course – the ultimate in tasty mood elevators! I have jazzed up one of my favorite desserts from childhood for a quick pick-me-up for a sad Crab. We always called this a cake although it is more of a pudding so I am interchanging the words here. Hope Cancer doesn't worry about that.

2 boxes chocolate pudding
  (or see chocolate pudding recipe page 98)
3 large firm bananas
2 tablespoons butter
2 tablespoons brown sugar

Serves 6

1 tablespoon dark rum – optional
8–10 ladyfingers
1 cup whipping cream
¼ cup semisweet chocolate, grated

Either prepare the chocolate pudding below or 2 boxes of chocolate pudding according to instructions on the box. Set it aside to cool.

Slice ½ of the bananas into ¼ inch rounds. In a medium sauté pan over low heat combine the butter and brown sugar. When the sugar is dissolved, stir in the rum and then place the bananas in the mixture in a single layer. Cook the bananas for 1 minute on each side. Take out of the pan and cool on a platter, again laying the bananas out in a single layer.

Line the bottom and sides of a 1 quart baking dish with the ladyfingers.

Beat the whipping cream in a large bowl with an electric beater until stiff. Fold all of the cream except ⅛ cup into the pudding but don't over-blend; you want to see the streaks of white through the chocolate.

Pour half of the pudding mixture into the baking dish. Layer the bananas on top – I like a triple layer of bananas. Pour the rest of the chocolate on top. Refrigerate until firm, at least 3 hours. (This can be made 1 day ahead. Cover and keep refrigerated.) Slice more bananas on top.

Dollop the remaining whipped cream on top and then sprinkle with the grated chocolate. If serving immediately you can slice some bananas on top too.

A note on brown bananas: bananas begin to decompose as soon as you peel them. Oxygen is the enemy of pretty, white bananas on the top of your dish. Either cut them just as you are about to serve the pudding, or put the bananas into a bowl with a teaspoon of fresh lemon juice and coat them well. This will slow the oxidation process. In either case, cover the pudding with plastic wrap until you are ready to cut into it.

Chocolate Pudding

½ pound semi-sweet chocolate
2 cups whole milk (you can do skim but it will be more watery)
¼ cup sugar
⅛ cup cornstarch
1 teaspoon pure vanilla extract

Serves 6

Fill the bottom of a double boiler with water, place the chocolate in the top part and place over medium heat. Gently stir the chocolate occasionally as it melts. Remove to a large pot (unless your double boiler is big enough) and carefully stir in milk, sugar and cornstarch until the sugar and starch are melted and all of the ingredients are incorporated. Remove from the heat and stir in the extract.

Pour into a large bowl, place plastic wrap on the surface of the pudding (to prevent pudding skin) and refrigerate at least 4 hours or overnight.

Opposites Attract: Stretching your Cancer South Node

The opposite sign from Moon Child is Capricorn.

Where Moon Child is all about hearth, home and

nation, Capricorn is interested in things such as

world politics and international relations. I am

paying homage to the ruler of Moon Child, the

Moon, while still asking these children of the

Moon to be comfortable in someone else's

living room for a change with this Pad Thai

recipe on page 100.

Pad Thai with Shrimp

Pad Thai Sauce

> ½ teaspoon tamarind paste
> ¼ cup chicken stock
> 4 tablespoons fish sauce
> 1 tablespoon soy sauce
> 1 teaspoon cayenne pepper
> 4 tablespoons brown sugar

Pad Thai

> 10 ounces Thai rice noodles
> 3 tablespoons soy sauce
> 2 cups cooked chicken breast, cubed
> 2 tablespoons vegetable oil
> 3 garlic cloves, diced
> 1 fresh red chili pepper, minced
> ¼–½ cup chicken stock
> 4 cups bean sprouts
> 1 pound medium shrimp, clean and deveined
> 4 spring onions, sliced
> ½ cup fresh cilantro
> ⅓ cup peanuts, chopped
> Juice of 1 lime
> 2 limes, wedged
>
> Serves 4

For the sauce, stir all of the ingredients in a small bowl until the sugar and tamarind paste are dissolved. If you really like it hotter add more tamarind or 1 teaspoon freshly ground black pepper. Cover and refrigerate.

Bring 3 quarts of water to a boil in a large sauté pan over high heat and immediately remove from the heat. Toss in the rice noodles and let them soak for about 3 minutes. Drain and rinse with cold water. Set aside.

Place the chicken cubes in a small bowl. Pour the soy sauce over the chicken and stir well. Heat the oil in a large frying pan (or wok if you have one) over medium heat. Add the garlic and red chili, stir for about 1 minute. Raise the heat to high and add the marinated chicken. Add the chicken stock 1 tablespoon at a time to keep the chicken from drying out. Slowly Air Signs – slowly! Cook for about 8–10 minutes. Lower the heat to medium. Immediately add the noodles and the Pad Thai sauce. Gently – gently incorporate the noodles until everything is combined. Do not break or mash the noodles Fire Signs! Cook another 2 minutes.

Add the bean sprouts and shrimp and cook 2–3 minutes, until the shrimp turn pink. The noodles are done when they are sticky.

Gently place the mixture onto a serving plate. Top with the onions, cilantro and peanuts. Squeeze some lime over top and decorate with the wedges. Serve immediately.

A note about Oriental noodles: Don't be afraid of making Oriental noodles. So many of us think that these dishes are so exotic… if you can cook pasta you can cook a rice noodle. All you are doing is substituting. Have fun with food, don't fear it

Dessert

Gram's Cranberry Pie

Every Christmas my friend, Diane Stoy, makes her Gram's cranberry pie as a way to keep her grandmother's memory alive. It is a wonderful tradition – to be appreciated by tradition-bound Cancer, and a very good pie!

This is what Diane has to say about her Gram's pie. "So you thought cranberries were only for use in cranberry sauce?? Here is a famous original recipe for cranberry. Gram lives on in many ways, but especially in this recipe. Over the years, her granddaughter shared this special treat with many others in Washington, D.C. Now this delicious memory can be enjoyed by friends everywhere. Thanks, Gram!"

1 ¼ cup fresh cranberries, washed
1 cup sugar, divided
1 egg (2 eggs if you want a fluffier batter)
¼ cup butter, melted
½ cup flour
⅛ teaspoon baking powder
¼ cup walnuts or pecans (optional. Diane leaves these little buggers out when she brings this to my house.)
1 cup whipping cream or vanilla ice cream (optional)

Makes one 8-inch pie

Preheat the oven to 325 degrees.

Place the cranberries in a plate and sprinkle with ¼ cup of the sugar. In a large bowl mix all of the other ingredients well except the ice cream or whipped cream and pour on top of the berries. (Batter may be thick.) Bake for 45 minutes in a greased 8-inch pie plate. Serve warm or cold with the whipped cream or plain.

To serve with the whipped cream just beat the cream with an electric blender until it becomes cream and dollop on top.

You can also serve with vanilla ice cream.

A note on cranberries: They are usually in the stores only around the holidays. However, cranberries, like all berries freeze very well, so buy some extra and toss them into the freezer. Gram's pie is great with ice cream in summer too.

Famous People
with
Cancer South Node – Capricorn North Node

Oprah Winfrey –

You can see the nurturing Earth mother very clearly in Oprah. She has moved well into her Capricorn North Node by becoming a media mogul and an empire into herself really. (A very paternal thing to do.) She used the touchy-feely aspect of Cancer to build a Capricornian empire. Like many Cancerians she too has had to come to terms with foods that provide solace to the soul but pounds to the body.

Michael Moore –

How funny it is that someone moving into Capricorn in this lifetime should become an institution by knocking the great institutions of American life. I believe this is a case of someone using his South Node, Cancer, the mother-protector-nurturer, to go after those who he feels have abandoned that role and the people for whom they should care. Perhaps in his next life, after he has worked out this angst, he will be a very compassionate government leader. He has spoken about his problems with food. Again, he is a Cancer-influenced person seeking solace in comfort foods.

Cancer rising David Bowie's favorite food is said to be plantains
roasted over an open fire. That sounds to me very homey –
very sitting around the campfire – very Cancerian.

leo

Chapter 7

Ah, Leo the King of the jungle the lover of all things splendid and comfortable. Leo cares more than its fellow Fire Sign Aries ever will about the well-being of others, although they can be a bit dismissive and a bit fussy. After all, the King must care and provide for his subjects – IF they pay him the proper homage that is. While some Leos eat like King Henry VIII, thinking their kingliness will keep them always healthy and svelte no matter what the scale and the doctors say – many more are so conscious of how they appear to their subjects that they are secret scale watchers. I have done my best to appeal to the narcissistic and epicurious sides of our lovely Lion with these creations.

Leo is happiest in the 5th house and vibrates to the energy in the 5th which relates to all forms of creativity and how we express ourselves. Leo is ruled by the Sun and they love to shine. Children, fun and play are all elements that capture 5th house energy.

Positive aspects of Leo include:
warmth, gregariousness and the ability to be a welcoming host as well as a great parent.

Shadow aspects of Leo include:
narcissism, arrogance, pettiness and haughtiness.

Foodie aspects of Leo include:
the ability to spread a beautiful table for guests, a taste for luxury as well as the taste for diet food when alone.

Famous People with Leo Rising

Donald Trump – Yes, you can always recognize a Leo rising by his or her mane. Even when they resort to comb-overs that become caricatures, they will do their darndest to preserve their mane. Oh yeah and he might have a touch of Leo arrogance. I understand that his favorite foods are sirloin steak or T bone, which must be served exactly the way he wants with no veggies or starches. Personally, I think he would be a much nicer person if he had more roughage, but the Leo the King eats the way he insists!

Lucille Ball – She dyed her mane bright red so everyone would see it. Her innate Leo dignity came through despite all of her clowning. Ms. Ball was a double Leo – Leo Sun and Leo Rising. She created some of the most hysterical television scenes using food as props. My personal favorite was when she went to work in a chocolate factory and I read that she considered chocolate one of her favorite foods. That is fitting for Leo, since chocolate was often considered a food of the gods and kings.

Appetizer

Smoked Salmon Paté with Caviar

This salmon pate' is a great example of balancing elegance with dietary considerations because it can be made low-fat and low-carb. Pate' is a perfect Leonean food and if you are a Leo on a budget – perish the thought – this works just as well without the caviar. You can decorate with sprigs of rosemary.

¾ pound smoked salmon
¾ cup mascarpone cheese (or cream cheese if you can't find it)
2 tablespoons lemon juice
¼ cup green onions, minced
2 ½ ounces salmon roe
24 pumpernickel rounds*
½ cup crème fraiche (optional)
1 ounce red caviar

Serves 8

Puree the salmon, cheese and lemon juice in a food processor and then pulse in the onions until mixed thoroughly. Stir in the roe. Scoop the salmon mixture on top of the bread rounds or cucumbers. Drop a dollop of the crème fraiche on top if you are using it and spoon the caviar over it and serve immediately.

*1–2 seedless cucumbers, sliced into ⅛-inch slices, can be substituted for the pumpernickel rounds if you are going low-carb.

You can also serve the pate in ramekins and allow your guests to make their own rounds on the bread or cucumber.

Caviar and roe are very similar. if you can't find both just use one but the difference of the 2 tastes makes this dish more special.

Soup

Cream of Wild Mushroom Soup

I have made this soup for Christmas several times and it is always an elegant winner. I am lucky to have several great farmers markets near me where I can get an assortment of wonderful wild mushrooms. I have tried many different kinds over the years and these work best for me. Try to get the hen of the woods; it really makes this soup wonderful! Go with the mushrooms you have – but the more wild the better. Morels work well too.

8 tablespoons unsalted butter
1 cup white onions, diced
2 large leeks, chopped
1 teaspoon fresh thyme, minced
1 teaspoon each kosher salt and
freshly ground black pepper
8 ounces shitake mushrooms
8 ounces oyster or cremini mushrooms

Serves 8

8 ounces hen of the woods mushrooms
5 cups chicken stock,
   (see page 44 for homemade stock)
1 cup white wine or for a sweeter taste a dry sherry
2 cups milk* (you can use 2 percent but it won't
   be as creamy)
½ cup flat-leaf Italian parsley, minced

I know they look nasty when dirty, but you can't really wash mushrooms. They soak up the water and lose any taste and then the water leeches out during cooking and makes the soup wimpy. Give them a good going over with a wet paper towel to clean. (If you have a heavily Air or Fire Sign dominated family go find some good Earth Sign friends for this chore. Patience is usually a pain to me, but in this case it is virtuous.) Cut the mushrooms into bite-size pieces. You can use the stems of most mushrooms except the shitakes.

Place the butter in a large soup pan over medium heat. Don't make the heat too high as the butter will burn. As the butter starts to melt add the onions, leeks and spices and cook for about 15 minutes, until the onions are getting soft and brown. Add the mushrooms and cook until they start to brown – about 7 minutes. You may have to add a few teaspoons of additional butter or drop in some olive oil if the mixture is getting dry.

Remove about 8 ounces of mushrooms from the pan and set aside.

Pour in the chicken stock, being sure to scrape the bottom of the pot to "deglaze" – get up all of the bits that might be sticking. Stir in the wine and bring back to a boil, stirring often.

Remove from the heat. Puree with an immersion blender or food processor. (If you have an immersion blender be sure not to have the hot liquid splash in your face.)

Return to the pot and heat. Stir in milk, stirring often until it has returned to a boil.

Before serving sprinkle the parsley and remaining mushrooms on top. Serve hot.

*You can use 1 cup milk and 1 cup heavy cream but it makes it very rich and adds calories.

A note on mushrooms: If you must wash them, here is one way to get all of the water out before you ruin your dish. Wash them quickly, dry on paper towels. Heat a medium sauté pan over very low heat. Put the mushrooms in the pan in a single layer – don't crowd. Leave them on the heat until no more water comes out. Keep your heat low and turn them gently once or twice.

Lobster Ravioli with Mushroom and Sage Cream Sauce

Some of my most enduring memories are of making ravioli with my mother. I remember making a "well" on the kitchen counter with mounds of flour and chasing after the escaping eggs with my hands as she cracked them into the center of the well. She didn't use pasta machines or pastry cutters. Her cutter was a four-inch round glass – which I still have – and she used the blunt end of a nut pick to hold the ravioli together. These common tools worked just fine. We always had a ricotta cheese filling but try this lobster filling to impress your Lion. Besides, the Leo who deigns to cook will secretly love playing in the dough.

Don't drown the ravioli in the cream sauce – the lobster is rich enough!

You can go ahead and cook the lobster yourself but it will taste almost as good if you buy it cleaned and ready to go!

> 8 tablespoons unsalted butter
> ½ cup fresh fennel bulb, diced
> 3 garlic cloves, minced
> 3 pounds fresh lobster meat, diced
> ½ cup fresh flat-leaf Italian parsley, minced
> 1 teaspoon each kosher salt and
>   freshly ground black pepper
> 20 sage leaves
> 1 tablespoon extra-virgin olive oil
>
> Serves 8

For Sauce
> 4 tablespoons unsalted butter
> 10 ounces shitake mushrooms, diced
> 3 garlic cloves, minced
> 1 teaspoon each kosher salt and
>   freshly ground black pepper
> 1 cup heavy cream

For dough
> 3 cups all-purpose flour
> 4 eggs
> 3 tablespoons kosher salt, divided
> 1 teaspoon extra-virgin olive oil

Put the butter in a medium sauté pan over medium heat. As it melts add the fennel, sauté for about 8 minutes until soft and starting to brown, add the garlic and cook for another minute. Add the lobster meat, being sure that it is mixed with the fennel and garlic – you don't want any lumps. Stir in the parsley, salt and pepper and cook for another 5 minutes. Set aside to cool. If you aren't going to make your dough for several hours be sure to refrigerate this mixture.

Wash the fresh sage leaves and dry thoroughly on paper towel. Don't crush them; you want whole leaves. Heat the olive oil in a medium sauté pan; add the leaves and cook for 5–7 seconds. Remove from oil onto clean paper towels and allow to cool.

This is a good time to make the sauce. In a medium soup pan over medium melt the butter, add the mushrooms and sauté for about 7 minutes until the mushrooms are turning brown. Add the garlic, salt and pepper and cook another 3 minutes. Pour in the heavy cream, stirring to deglaze the mushroom bits. Just before serving bring the sauce back up to a low boil.

Now to the dough: pour the flour onto a clean counter top or marble pastry board. Make a "well" or hole in the center with flour walls all around. Crack the eggs into the well – be careful to watch for any running out of the well – just direct it back to the center. Sprinkle with 1 tablespoon of salt and add the oil to eggs. With a swirling action begin to mix the eggs into the flour. As the egg and flour blend together work the dough until it is slightly sticky. Don't knead the dough or beat it to death. Be gentle and leave a bit of stickiness to the dough – it shouldn't be sticking to your hands but not be totally dry. Less work is more here. (I see you smiling over that Taurus.)

Wrap the dough in plastic wrap – Mom used a dish towel; – if you use a towel be sure it is wrapped well so no air creeps in – and let it rest on the cabinet for 20 minutes.

Work with the dough in halves so it doesn't dry out. Cut it in half – and keep the other half wrapped until ready to roll out. Roll out the dough on a clean counter top that has been lightly dusted with flour – or use your pasta machine. Dough should be ⅛ inch thick.

If you have a fancy pastry cutter use it – as I said Mom's 4-inch glass works well. Scoop about ⅓ of a tablespoon of filling into 1 cut out round – place another round over top and with your hands fit it tightly over the filling to remove any air pockets. Be careful – don't make any holes in the top dough. Fold the edges of the bottom piece over the top part and get your trusty nut pick to pinch the 2 edges together so the ravioli won't open when cooked.

To cook the ravioli, fill a large soup pot with about 8 quarts of water, sprinkle in 2 tablespoons salt and 1 teaspoon olive oil. Bring the water to a rolling boil over medium-high heat. Drop the ravioli in one by one carefully and cook about 3–4 minutes each. In the meantime pour the sauce into a large serving bowl.

When the ravioli is cooked, drain out water and immediately gently toss the ravioli in the bowl with the sauce. Gently turn the ravioli to coat in the sauce. Place the sage leaves on top of the ravioli and serve immediately.

Veggies & Fruit

Acorn Squash Stuffed with Apples, Figs and Grapes

Acorn squash was considered primitive by early settlers in America because it was favored by Native Americans. Made with figs and grapes it would be satisfying even to the palate of Henry VIII. The juxtaposition of rough squash and elegant figs will appeal to the child in Leo.

2 large acorn squash, halved and seeded
2 tablespoons butter
1 cup green apples, cored, diced and skinned
1 cup dried figs, diced
1 cup green grapes, halved
1 cup raisins

Serves 4

½ cup white wine
3 tablespoons honey
1 teaspoon kosher salt
1 teaspoon freshly ground black pepper
1 teaspoon cinnamon
1 teaspoon freshly grated nutmeg

Preheat the oven to 400 degrees.

In a medium saucepan melt the butter over low heat. Add the apples, figs, grapes, raisins, wine and honey and cook slowly, stirring often, until the wine has evaporated. Spoon the fig mixture into the acorn squash and sprinkle the salt, pepper, cinnamon and nutmeg over the squash.

If you have already cooked the squash, cook for 20 minutes until the squash is soft. If the squash is raw cook it for 45 minutes. Serve immediately.

A note on nutmeg: Treat yourself and go buy whole nutmeg cloves and a little grater. There is nothing like the taste of freshly ground nutmeg in any dish – and eggnog at the holidays.

A note on squash: I don't believe in destroying my hands to cut squash and I am not big fan of knives that can slice a giraffe in two on a single swipe. Sharp knives are important but I don't like handling lethal weapons. You can cut the squash in half and scoop out seeds when it is raw but if you want an easier way to handle all squash, toss them into the oven whole and let them get soft. Remove and let cool and then cut and seed.

Shrimp in Artichoke Cups

This is a very pretty and unique dish that the Leo will appreciate. While they make great hosts, in private Leos are very careful of their diets. The king must not be obese and must always make a good appearance before his subjects unless the Leo is in the position to cut off the heads of those who point and giggle, but that has sort of gone out of fashion lately.

6 large artichokes
1 lemon, cut in quarters
1 pound medium shrimp, cleaned and deveined
¼ cup extra-virgin olive oil
2 teaspoons fresh thyme, chopped
½ teaspoon kosher salt
1 teaspoon red pepper flakes

Serves 6

For Sauce

1 garlic clove, minced
1 tablespoon horseradish
1 cup mayonnaise
½ cup chili sauce

Trim the tops off of the artichokes and cut about ¼ inch on each leaf to get the prickly portions off. Rub the cut parts of the artichoke with the lemon. Put the artichokes in a large microwave-safe dish, pour in ½ cup water in the bottom of the bowl and cover tightly with plastic wrap. (Don't pile them up – do this in batches if your microwave isn't big enough.) Cook on high for about 17 minutes. (If you divided the artichokes, cook for 10 minutes.) Let them sit for 5 minutes and then carefully remove the wrap. The artichokes should be soft; if not re-cover and cook another 5 minutes.

When the artichokes are cool, remove the fuzzy choke part in the center with a spoon and toss.

Preheat the oven to 375 degrees.

Place the shrimp, oil, and herbs into a baking dish in one layer and roast for about 10 minutes until pink. Remove from the oven and cool.

In a medium bowl mix all of the ingredients for the sauce until totally combined. Cover and refrigerate for 3–4 hours.

Just before you are ready to serve, fill the artichoke centers to slightly over ½ way up with the sauce. Hang 4–6 shrimp off of the lip of the artichoke. Scatter any remaining shrimp around the serving platter.

A note on shrimp: I love to roast shrimp for almost every recipe. It just adds a deep flavor. Just place them in a baking dish with olive oil, garlic, salt and pepper and roast them for a few minutes. You will taste the difference.

Meat & Fish

Roasted Swan, Pheasant, Crane or... Something a Bit More Modern

Pomegranate and Orange Glazed Cornish Hens with Oyster Stuffing

I have to honor the royalty of Leo and my love of history with this dish. I found a basic recipe in an old medieval cookery book years ago and have worked to modernize it. If you can't go out and have your minions shoot a pheasant or swan on your kingly estate, go buy some Cornish hens.

Cornish hens are small. If you have big eaters then judge one per person. More genteel folk will do fine with half a hen. This recipe assumes half a hen per person.

In the good old days they would put the stuffing in the birds but it just makes them way too dry.

1 cup butter, softened
4 tablespoons fresh herbs – thyme, chives and rosemary
   work best but use what you like, minced
4 Cornish hens
10 tablespoons each kosher salt and
   freshly ground black pepper
8 lemons, cut into quarters
4 cinnamon sticks
8 pieces star anise
½ cup pomegranate juice
1 cup orange juice
6 tablespoons honey or agave nectar

Serves 8

4 large carrots
1 cup white wine
1 cup chicken stock
   (see page 44 for homemade recipe)
1 ½ pounds of sausage out of casings
   (hot or mild is up to your taste.)
1 large white onion, diced
5 celery stalks, diced
15 oysters, shucked*
1 tablespoon flat-leaf Italian parsley, minced
1 tablespoon fresh thyme, minced

Preheat the oven to 375 degrees.

Mix the butter and herbs together in a small bowl until well blended.

Remove any giblets from the hens. (You can add these to the stuffing if you sauté them well and then chop them up. I am not a big fan of giblets, but in a good stuffing they do add a flavor without tasting like sawdust as they so often do.) Wash the hens well and pat dry inside and out. Salt and pepper the cavity liberally. Carefully pull the skin away from the flesh of the birds and insert a generous amount of the butter/herb mixture, known as a compound butter, in the pocket you are creating. Do not tear the skin but, Capricorns, there is no need to get out a slide rule and measure each pocket to 1000 of an inch. Stuff the lemons into the cavity of the birds along with the cinnamon sticks and star anise.

In a small saucepan heat the pomegranate and orange juices and honey over low heat for 5 minutes until the juice reduces and starts to thicken.

Place the carrots on the bottom of a large roasting pan and place the birds on top, breast side up. Pour ½ cup of the wine and chicken stock into the bottom of the pan. Cook the birds for 25 minutes and then brush on some of the glaze. Cook another 15 minutes, glaze the breasts again and then turn the birds over, glaze again and return to the oven. Cook until a meat thermometer inserted into the thigh reads 165 degrees – about another 30–40 minutes.

When they are done, remove from the oven, cover with aluminum foil and let rest for about 30 minutes. Always let your meat rest before serving.

While the hens are cooking make the stuffing. Cook the sausage in a large skillet until browned. Remove to a paper towel to cool. Drain all but 1 tablespoon of fat out of the pan. Add the onions and celery and sauté over medium heat until soft – about 6 minutes. Add the oysters, parsley and thyme and cooked sausage. Stir in the rest of the white wine and cook until wine is absorbed and all ingredients are mixed well.

Serve the birds on a bed of the stuffing. Spoon some of the wine/stock mixture from the pan over top. You can dress them up with some grapes and figs displayed around the dish to make them look more elegant.

*You can buy jars of shucked oyster meats – 1 16-ounce jar works here. Or you can get oysters "shell stocked" – basically sold live on a ½ shell. Remember, you have to work fast with these, so don't leave them around the refrigerator for a few days. Take them home and get to work.

A note on tearlessly chopping onions: Put them in the freezer for 15 minutes before cutting. A cold onion is a less-weepy onion. You can also do the cutting near a running kitchen vent so the fumes go up the vent and not in your face.

Poached Salmon in Parchment

The parchment wrap makes this dish look like a little present that you are setting before the king, Leo the Lion. If there is one thing the king loves it is presents from his loyal subjects. Remember Leo vibrates to the 5th house, the house of children and creativity and they like to act like kids. When no one is looking! Of course, they prefer big presents but you will win them over with the taste of this dish.

½ stick unsalted butter
3 cups red or green bell peppers, cut into thin strips
½ cup leeks, cut into strips
2 cups fresh tomatoes, sliced thinly
5 tablespoons fresh basil, minced
1 teaspoon kosher salt

Serves 8

1 teaspoon red pepper flakes
2 teaspoons fresh fennel fronds, chopped
8 5-ounce pieces skinless wild salmon
3 tablespoons extra-virgin olive oil
8 12-inch squares parchment paper

Preheat the oven to 400 degrees.

Heat the butter in a large skillet and add the peppers and leeks, cook over medium heat until they start to become soft – about 4 minutes. Add the tomatoes and cook until most of the tomato juice is gone, another 4–5 minutes. You don't want soggy packets but don't burn them! Stir in the basil, salt, pepper and fennel and remove from the heat to cool.

Brush the salmon filets with the olive oil and place 1 in the center of the each parchment paper. Cover the tops of each salmon with a layer of the vegetable mixture. Fold each piece of parchment over the fish, making several folds as you go until the fish fillets are tightly sealed.

Place the salmon packets on an ungreased cookie sheet and bake 15–18 minutes. You can serve the salmon in the packets and let the guests reveal the surprise. (But make a little slit on top just before serving so the Leo doesn't burn his royal fingers and you don't have to hear the lion roar.)

A note on wild salmon: Is it worth buying wild salmon? Yes! Farmed salmon contains lots of Omega 6 which is actually not healthy. It is the Omega 3 of wild salmon that is good for us. Also, wild salmon tastes much, much better.

To Their Health

Healthy, Elegant Snapper

Leo rules the heart area, the arteries and the spine. Many Leos (depending on the placement of the sign in their chart) have the self-discipline and narcissism to take care of themselves. However, those who indulge too much at one of their many parties should watch the cardiovascular area.

This snapper dish will still appeal to the dignity of the Leo, but will come in handy when over-indulging and too much entertaining has taken the tool on their systems.

4 tablespoons extra-virgin olive oil, divided
2 cups plum tomatoes, quartered
½ cup fresh basil leaves, torn into small strips
1 tablespoon fresh oregano, chopped
8 large Italian green olives, pitted and chopped
¼ cup black olives
¼ cup capers
¼ teaspoon cinnamon

Serves 4

2 medium white onions, diced
3 garlic cloves, diced
4 snapper fillets, with skin
3 teaspoons kosher salt
1 teaspoon freshly ground black pepper
1 teaspoon red pepper flakes (optional)
½ cup white wine

Preheat the oven to 350 degrees.

Toss the tomatoes with 1 tablespoon of the olive oil. Spread out on a baking sheet and roast 15 minutes. Transfer tomatoes to a medium bowl and toss with the basil, oregano, cinnamon, olives and capers.

In a medium skillet over medium heat, sauté the onions until they start to soften and start getting brown – about 10 minutes. Add the garlic and sauté another 2 minutes. Don't burn the garlic. Add the garlic and onions to tomato mixture.

Dry the fish well with a paper towel and then rub each fillet with the rest of the olive oil and season with salt and pepper. If you want more of a kick, season with the red pepper flakes.

Heat the same skillet over medium
heat and place the fish in skin side
down; cook for about 4–6 minutes.
Flip and cook for another 4–6
minutes. The fish should flake easily.
Remove to a side dish.

Deglaze the pan with the wine and
let it cook down to about half of the
original amount. Place the vegetables
back in the pan just to heat them up
and then place over the fish. Pour
any remaining wine over the top
and serve immediately.

Opposites Attract: Stretching Your Leo South Node

Most Leos love to entertain. Despite their lordliness they make elegant hosts and really care about the comfort of their "subjects." The sign opposite Leo is Aquarius, which epitomizes the equality and humanity of all people. There are no class divisions with Aquarius. To help ease Leo into the transition, try this elegant pulled pork wrap. Leo can tolerate something as messy as pulled pork if wrapped nicely and surrounded by baby field greens.

Pulled Pork with Field Greens

The meat should marinate overnight if possible so plan accordingly.

For Dry Rub

    5 tablespoons paprika
    2 tablespoons brown sugar
    3 tablespoons dry mustard
    2 tablespoons cayenne pepper
    3 tablespoons kosher salt
    7–9 pounds butt pork roast (or shoulder)
    1 head garlic, minced
    2 8-ounce cans beer

    Serves 12

Preheat the oven to 300 degrees.

For Barbecue Sauce

    1 cup apple cider vinegar
    ½ cup Dijon mustard
    ½ cup tomato paste
    ⅓ cup brown sugar
    1 teaspoon kosher salt
    ½ teaspoon freshly ground black pepper
    24–30 sandwich wraps, pita pockets or small rolls
    2 cups field greens, washed and well dried

Mix all of the dry rub ingredients in a small bowl and then rub all over the pork. (Don't add beer now!) Cover and refrigerate for at least 4 hours; overnight is better.

Place the pork into a deep roasting pan, pour the beer over it, cover with foil and roast it for about 6 hours. Check it every hour or so to be sure it hasn't dried out. Add some more beer, chicken stock, wine or even water to keep it moist. The pork should be tender to the point of falling apart.

While the pork is roasting, make the barbecue sauce. Combine all of the sauce ingredients in a medium saucepan over a medium heat. Simmer gently, stirring, for 15 minutes. Remove from the heat to cool.

When the pork is done, take it out of the oven and allow it to cool so you can handle it. I prefer to don plastic gloves and pull the pork apart with my hands. More genteel types (e.g. Leo, Taurus and Virgo) will prefer to take 2 forks and pull the pork apart. Shred the pork, removing any fat and gristle. Pour the barbeque sauce over the shredded pork and mix well so that the pork is coated.

An hour before you are going to serve, return the pork to the oven to heat thoroughly; this should take 30 minutes. You want the pork warm but not so hot that it will destroy the field greens. If it looks dry, pour in a little more liquid but don't make it soggy.

While the pork is reheating, wash and thoroughly dry the field greens. Lay out the wraps. With a fork place a layer of the pork in the middle of an open wrap. Add a layer of field greens and roll up.

ЯЯЯ♈♉♊♋♌♍♎♏♐♑♒♓

Individual Baked Alaskas

When I was a kid back in the Stone Age, Baked Alaska was the coolest dessert going. I just thought it was so great – hot and cold with meringue on top. Get out of town! It sort of went "out of flavor" in the '70s and '80s but I think it is time to bring it back and who better to bring back an old classic with a flair for the dramatic than Leo? I like the idea of individual Alaskas for the Leo – as they can be a bit territorial.

I like to put the shortcake shells in the freezer for 24 hours so plan accordingly.

Meringue:

6 egg whites
¼ teaspoon cream of tartar
6 ounces sugar
¼ teaspoon pure vanilla extract
¼ teaspoon salt

6 shortcake shells*
1 pint vanilla ice cream**
 – make sure this is frozen really hard.

Serves 6

Again, this won't work unless the ice cream is frozen hard. Place the shortcake shells in the freezer 24 hours before making this dessert.

Preheat the oven to 450 degrees.

For the meringue, beat the egg whites until foamy and then slowly add the rest of the ingredients until soft peaks form.

Keep the ice cream in the freezer until ready to use. Scoop the ice cream into the center of the cake shells and cover each with a layer of meringue about ½ inch thick. For an extra Leo flair bring the meringue to a small peak on top.

Bake 3 minutes until the meringue has browned lightly. Serve immediately.

*If you are a Cancer and wish to use grandma's individual shortcake recipe to make your own, be my guest. I am too much an impatient Gemini South Node for that!

**To be more colorful you can use ½ pint vanilla and ½ pint strawberry ice cream and put ½ scoop of each on the shells.

Dessert

Famous People with
Leo South Node – Aquarius North Node

Elvis Presley –

"The King" who, in fine Leo fashion, was known for his distinctive haircut and I think he sang, too! Elvis embodied a great deal of his Leo South Node qualities. Yet, he was also known for doing many things such as giving away cars and houses, which clearly showed he was embracing his Aquarian North Node aspects. Of course, Elvis had "food issues." While his tastes were more Aquarian than Leo – peanut butter and banana sandwiches being on the top of his long list of favorites – he was very Leo-like in his refusal to stop gorging.

Joseph Stalin –

I use him as an example of how much we can build up shadow aspects of our South Node if we refuse to move and get karmicly stuck. There was nothing Aquarian about this dogmatic, brutal dictator. Stalin ate like the king he thought he was and his large, late night dinners were legendary. Some of his favorite dishes included heavy lamb casseroles and mince cakes.

Jon Bon Jovi has opened Soul Kitchen in New Jersey – a "pay-what-you-can" restaurant for people who are on limited incomes. I can't think of a more gracious, "kingly" act from this Leo North Node.

virgo
Chapter 8

People with a strong Virgo influence are all about healthy eating. Virgo vibrates to the 6th house – the house of taking care of the physical body and health and day-to-day "nose to the grindstone" work. Someone with a lot of Virgo in their chart will take to the Earth to find their food – organic being all the better. It is all about healthy food – easily prepared in a common sense way.

Virgo has just found her ruler. For years, she was given Mercury as her planetary ruler, which frankly never made a lot of sense to me. Virgos are not fast moving quick thinkers – at all! They are methodical and dutiful. Many modern astrologers have found her a new ruler in the asteroid Vesta, the dutiful worker who selflessly kept the hearth fires burning. Vesta is all about self-effacing duty –working correctly, eating correctly and being correct in so many ways. Yeah, that is Virgo, always on the search for perfection.

Positive aspects of Virgo include:
organizational abilities, precision, hard work and caring for their diets.

Shadow aspects of Virgo include:
hyper-criticism, self-doubt and the unyielding quest for perfection
in everyone and everything around them, especially themselves.

Foodie aspects of Virgo include:
simple, healthy, plain food and farm-to-table food.

Famous People with Virgo Rising

Woody Allen – Well, I guess you would say he would have a bit of a hyper critical personality and just a smidge of self-doubt. His Virgo persnicketiness is typified in a quote often attributed to him, "I will not eat oysters. I want my food dead. Not sick, not wounded: dead."

Agatha Christie – Dame Agatha's use of herbs and poisons as murder weapons for many of her killers is a very Virgoan act. She was known for being dedicated to her work, churning out a huge library of books. She wrote about food, of course, in her books but little is written about her food likes and dislikes, other than she liked apples. With Virgo Sun and Virgo rising it is not unusual that she would prefer a simple fruit.

Appetizer

Carrot Chips with Orange Yogurt Dip

Carrots and yogurt: most people won't find that too exciting a combination but it will be music to the ears of healthy, practical Virgo. These chips are baked – not fried, of course, no fried for Virgo, and are quite good despite what less health conscious signs might think. Yes, I am talking to you, Scorpio and Taurus.

7 large carrots, scraped
3 teaspoons extra-virgin olive oil
1 teaspoon kosher salt
For dip
16 ounces plain Greek yogurt
   – please always go Greek when you are
   going yogurt – it is so much richer in texture

¼ cup orange juice
2 tablespoons honey
⅛ cup coconut, grated

Serves 6

Preheat the oven to 350 degrees.

If you are feeling fancy you can slice the carrots into ½ inch slices with one of those Y shaped vegetable peelers or a mandolin or you can slice them in half lengthwise. Place them into a medium size bowl and add the oil and salt. Mix well, preferably with your hands (Virgo put on some plastic gloves if you have to.) Place the carrots in a single layer on an ungreased baking sheet and bake about 20–30 minutes, until they start to turn golden brown.

While the carrots are cooking, mix all of the ingredients for the dip except the coconut in a medium bowl and mix well. Place the dip in a serving bowl and sprinkle the coconut on top. Serve alongside the carrots as soon as they have cooled to room temperature.

♈ ♉ ♊ ♋ ♌ ♍ ♎ ♏ ♐ ♑ ♒ ♓

Soup

Corn Soup

This is a wonderful summer soup when your Virgo can pick the fresh corn and then head to the kitchen. It is uncomplicated and pure – other aspects the Virgo will also enjoy.

4 ears fresh corn
2 tablespoons butter
1 large white onion, chopped
1 large carrot, diced
1 celery stalk, diced
2 garlic cloves, minced
3 teaspoons fresh thyme, minced
2 teaspoons fresh rosemary sprigs, minced
1 teaspoon freshly ground black pepper
1 teaspoon kosher salt
3 cups low-fat milk

Serves 8

For topping:

1 tablespoon extra-virgin olive oil
4 chili peppers, cut in half
¼ cup cooked corn kernels
1 tablespoon cilantro, minced
(if you hate cilantro like I do, go with parsley)

Heat 2 quarts of water in a medium saucepan over high heat. Clean and husk the corn. Gently add the corn to the water and boil it for about 4 minutes. Remove from the heat carefully with tongs and place in a large dish of cold water.

Melt the butter in a large soup pot over low heat. Add the onion and caramelize – about 15–30 minutes, stirring often. Add the carrot, celery, garlic and herbs; cook until the veggies are lightly browned – about 5 minutes.

When the corn is cool, remove the kernels from the cob. The best way to do this is to place the cob in the center of a Bundt pan. Hold one end with a kitchen towel and use a paring knife to scrape the kernels into the body of Bundt pan. No muss (Virgo will like that), no fuss.

Add the corn and milk to the pot and raise the heat to medium-high. Bring the soup to a boil, stirring often. Shut off the heat and let it cool. If you have an immersion blender, insert it into the pot and blend until the soup is smooth. Or pulse in a food processor until smooth.

The soup can be stored in the refrigerator for a day or two.

Just before serving, heat the oil in a medium sauté pan over medium heat, add the peppers and cilantro and cook until the peppers begin to brown – about 3 minutes.

Heat the soup in the soup pot over medium heat until warmed, stirring often. Top with a dollop of the pepper topping and serve immediately.

Pasta Primavera

Fresh, fresh, fresh veggies with a fresh tomato sauce are music to Virgo's ears. They will also like the precision of cutting the veggies. You can use quinoa or wheat pasta in the place of regular pasta as the veggies can stand up to the rougher taste of them.

2 pounds cherry tomatoes, cut in half
1 large bunch fresh basil leaves
4 teaspoons kosher salt, divided
¼ cup extra-virgin olive oil
1 pound fresh asparagus, cut into 1 inch strips
5 carrots, cleaned and cut into 1 inch strips
2 red bell peppers, cut into 1 inch strips

1 cup canned peas
12 ounces green beans
3 garlic cloves, minced
½ teaspoon dried hot red pepper flakes
1 pound farfalle pasta
¾ cup Parmigiano-Reggiano cheese, grated

Serves 6

A note on asparagus: Asparagus will tell you where to cut them. Just hold them with an end in each hand and snap. The tougher part will break from the more tender area. Cook the tender part and use the other for veggie stocks.

In a large bowl combine the tomatoes, basil and 2 teaspoons of the salt. Stir gently and quickly. Leave the bowl on the kitchen counter, uncovered, for 3–5 hours. Virgos love to pick at food. They don't feel worthy to eat an entire meal so they pick and pick. Keep your Virgo from picking all the tomatoes out of the bowl until they have time to render their juices.

In a large sauté pan, heat the olive oil over medium heat; add all of the remaining vegetables, garlic and red pepper. Sauté until they are soft and lightly browned – about 10 minutes.

While the veggies are cooking, bring 3 quarts of water combined with 2 teaspoons of salt to a boil in a large soup pot over high heat. Add the farfalle and cook for about 8–10 minutes until *al dente*.

Pour the tomato mixture into the sauté pan and mix with the other veggies to heat.

Drain the farfalle and mix in with the veggies. Top with the cheese and serve immediately.

A note on zucchini: Don't go for the biggest ones in the bunch, they have the least taste. Smaller is better – for zucchini anyway. Look for firm squash with a moist stem end to get the best.

Veggies & Fruit

Fennel with Tomatoes, Artichokes and Olives

As I kid I only had fennel raw. "Fenorque" was a staple at every Italian American Thanksgiving table where I came from and I hated it. It wasn't until years later, when I ate fennel cooked in a tomato stock, that I realized I loved fennel! I have tried to recreate the "a ha fennel dish" and threw in a few more things to make it tasty like Kalamata olives and artichoke hearts. Virgos will appreciate the healthy fennel and the cleanness of this dish. Just don't tell them you used canned artichoke hearts. Sorry, but to me canned works better in this dish.

⅛ cup extra-virgin olive oil
1 medium white onion, diced
1 large fennel bulb, cored and diced
2 13.75-ounce cans artichoke hearts, drained
2 garlic cloves, diced
10 roasted plum tomatoes, quartered
   (or see page 21 for my roasted tomatoes)

Serves 6

½ cup white wine
1 teaspoon kosher salt
¼ teaspoon red pepper flakes
1 teaspoon fresh thyme, diced
¼ cup Kalamata olives

In a large sauté pan over medium heat warm the oil. Sauté the onion, fennel and artichokes for 15 minutes until the fennel is just starting to get soft. Add the garlic and sauté another 2 minutes. Stir in the tomatoes, cook for 3 minutes and add the wine, salt, pepper and thyme. Cook another 5 minutes over medium heat, the fennel should be soft but not limp. Stir in the olives and serve immediately.

A note on dried herbs: When herbs are growing like mad in summer, simply cut, wash and then dry them on paper towels in a single layer. They take about a week to dry by air. If you don't have room to lay them out, place the herbs on cookie sheets and put them into a 250 degree oven for about an hour. They should just start to dry. Store in airtight glass jars. They are good for one winter but don't keep them any longer than that as they lose flavor. Wash and freeze chives and parsley because they turn brown when dried.

Eggplant Stacks

The trick to these is to get the eggplant and tomato slices as close in size as possible. I like the little Japanese eggplants because they are sweet and can match up to the tomatoes easily. This will appeal to the precision of Virgo; just be sure they don't go all Monk on you, trying to make the eggplant and tomato slices match to one millionth of an inch of each other.

4 Japanese eggplants, sliced into ¼-inch rounds*
4–5 medium tomatoes – about the same size around
   as eggplants, sliced into ¼-inch rounds
¼ cup extra-virgin olive oil, divided
2 teaspoons kosher salt
2 teaspoons freshly ground black pepper
3 garlic cloves, diced

1 pound ground turkey
2 tablespoons balsamic vinegar
3 tablespoons fresh oregano, minced
3 tablespoons fresh thyme, minced
1 pound mozzarella cheese,
   sliced in ¼ inch rounds
12 4-inch sturdy rosemary spears

Serves 6

Place the eggplant and tomato slices, all but 2 teaspoons of the oil, salt and pepper into a large bowl. Be sure each slice is coated in oil. Cover and place in the refrigerator for 2 hours.

In a medium sauté pan over medium heat sauté the garlic about 2 minutes until it starts to brown. Add the ground meat and cook until browned – about 5 minutes.

Preheat the oven to 450 degrees.

On a flat baking sheet covered with aluminum foil place 1 layer of eggplant. Brush the tops with the balsamic vinegar. Sprinkle the oregano and thyme over the eggplant.

Top each piece of eggplant with a layer of ground turkey, then a slice of mozzarella and then a slice of tomato and top off with another slice of eggplant. Spear the rosemary in the middle of the stack to hold it together. Drizzle the remaining olive oil over the stacks.

Bake 20–30 minutes until the cheese is melted and eggplant is soft. Serve immediately.

A note on eggplant: Traditionally eggplant is sliced thin, salted and placed in a colander to drain for several hours. This allegedly goes back to the days when eggplant was supposed to have some "poisons" inside. I find it isn't necessary to do this if the eggplants are young, small and relatively seedless. If you have to do it, I always found Mom's way easiest. She would slice them into a colander, salt them generously, press a saucer on top of the eggplants and set them on the drain board near the sink so the juices flowed into the sink.

Meat & Fish

Trout with Bok Choy

This dish is not only healthy, but also makes a neat presentation. I can see the Virgo jumping for joy over that prospect. Even if your Virgo is a great cook, they won't admit it to themselves. Why interfere with all of that perfectly good self-criticism that Virgo excels at? This is so easy to make, the Virgo just might start to feel good about themselves. Maybe.

4 tablespoons soy sauce
1 teaspoon brown sugar
1 teaspoon five spice powder
½ cup orange juice
4 trout fillets
4 tablespoons ginger, sliced thinly, divided

Serves 4

2 teaspoons sesame oil
2 baby bok choy, sliced into long slices
1 large red chili pepper, diced
4 scallions, diced

Cut aluminum foil into squares large enough to wrap one piece of the fish in each.

In medium bowl, whisk together the soy sauce, sugar, five-spice powder and orange juice. Add the trout fillets and 2 tablespoons ginger, cover and refrigerate for 30 minutes.

Preheat the oven to 375 degrees.

Heat the sesame oil in a medium sauté pan over low heat; add the bok choy, chili pepper and scallions and sauté about 5-8 minutes until they are getting soft and lightly browned.

Place 1 piece of fish in each piece of foil, add a couple of teaspoons of the sauce over the fish and distribute the bok choy, chili pepper and scallions equally on top of each fish. Sprinkle the remaining ginger on the fish fillets.

Fold the foil completely around each piece of fish. Place the packets on a baking sheet and cook 25 minutes. Open the foil carefully and turn the fish out onto the serving plate.

Fish Tacos

Some tacos can be messy – something Virgo can't abide. These tacos stay nicely in their shells and obediently don't drip. Virgo loves obedience and orderliness. I prefer hard shells with this but you can opt for soft.

2 pounds mahi mahi or any firm white fish
2 tablespoons fajita seasoning
3 tablespoons fresh cilantro
  or fresh flat-leaf Italian parsley, diced
1 teaspoon kosher salt
2 teaspoons freshly ground black pepper
¾ pound cabbage, sliced thinly

1 tablespoon fresh lime juice
2 avocados, pitted and diced
12 hard taco shells
6 tablespoons reduced fat sour cream
3 lemons, cut into wedges

Serves 6

Preheat the oven to 350 degrees.

Spray a cookie sheet with olive oil spray. Season the fish on both sides with the fajita seasoning, cilantro, salt and pepper. Cook the fish 2–3 minutes on each side until it is flaky.

While the fish is cooking, combine in a small bowl the cabbage, lime juice and avocados and mix well.

Slice the fish to fit in the taco shells. Spread a thin layer of sour cream on the inside of the taco shells. Then add the fish and top with the cabbage mixture. Serve with lemon wedges.

A note on fish: Many people hate fish because it is always dry. Fish does not need to be incinerated. Simply cook it to an internal temperature of 145 degrees and it is ready to go.

Chocolate Raspberry Ramekins

We know that Virgo is all about health, sometimes too much so. The Virgo loves service and duty and keeping it all together, but they aren't very good about giving themselves a treat or any credit. Sometimes they just need something decadent and delightful for themselves. These chocolate raspberry ramekins are delicious. If the Virgo feels too guilty indulging themselves tell them that the "dark chocolate is good for you" and the "raspberry is a healthy fruit." That might allow them to do something nice for themselves for a just a second.

To Their Health

½ stick unsalted butter, softened
18 ounces dark chocolate
5 eggs
¼ cup sugar
1 teaspoon pure vanilla extract

Serves 6

1 teaspoon coffee
2 tablespoons Chambord
1 cup raspberries
½ cup whipping cream

Preheat the oven to 375 degrees.

Fill the bottom of a double boiler with water. Put the butter and chocolate in the top portion and place over low heat until the butter and chocolate are melted, stirring often. Remove from the heat and stir in the eggs, sugar, vanilla, coffee and Chambord. Stir until thoroughly combined.

Layer the bottom of each ramekin with the raspberries. Pour the chocolate mixture over the raspberries and bake 15 minutes.

While the ramekins are cooking, whip the cream with an electric blender until it forms stiff peaks.

Serve the ramekins warm with a dollop of cream. (If the Virgo protests, you can replace the cream with low fat vanilla yogurt but do try to sneak in the real stuff.)

Opposites Attract: Stretching Your Virgo South Node

As we now know, Virgos are big into self-

denial and frugality. However, they are

moving into the world of Pisces the Fish

— entering the big ocean of cosmic awareness

— so for them I am making one of my favorite

fish dishes. Not only is Cioppino delicious,

but it is meant to be shared with others and

is perfect for getting the somewhat lonely

Virgos out of their shells. It also evokes the

wonders of the deep sea, which is very Piscean

in nature. It might even move Virgo to write

a Piscean poem.

Cioppino

3 cups clam juice
Pinch of saffron
5 tablespoons extra-virgin olive oil
2 medium white onions, chopped
1 medium fennel bulb, chopped
4 large garlic cloves, chopped
2 tablespoons tomato paste
1 28-ounce can whole plum tomatoes, drained and chopped
2 cups white wine

½ cup fresh flat-leaf Italian parsley, chopped
1 teaspoon red pepper flakes
2 pounds clams
1 pound mussels, cleaned and debearded
1 pound cooked crab legs, cracked into 3–5 inch pieces
1 pound scallops
1 ½ pounds fish fillets (salmon, halibut, white fish), cubed
1 pound large shrimp, peeled and deveined
½ stick butter, softened

Serves 6

In a medium saucepan heat over medium-low heat the clam juice and saffron, simmer for a few minutes and take off of the heat.

In a very large soup pot, heat the oil and add the onions, fennel and garlic and sauté about 5 minutes until they are soft and begin to brown. Stir in the tomato paste, tomatoes, saffron, all of the clam juice and wine and cook over medium heat for 30–40 minutes until all of the ingredients are incorporated. Stir in the herbs.

Add the clams, mussels and crab legs first; cook for 5 minutes. Add the scallops and fish fillets and cook another 5–7 minutes. Add the shrimp and cook for another 5–7 minutes until the clams are open and the shrimp are just pink.

Add the butter and stir the fish together – remove and serve immediately.

Dessert

Healthy Oatmeal Topped Crumble

You can use almost any in-season fruit for this crumble. In summer use blueberries and peaches. In winter, 6 cups of pears or apples work just as well.

Fruit Mixture

> 6 cups peaches, peeled and sliced
> 1 cup fresh blueberries
> ¼ cup orange juice
> ½ cup agave nectar
> ⅛ teaspoon freshly grated nutmeg
> 2 teaspoons cornstarch
>
> Serves 8

Preheat the oven to 400 degrees.

Bring all the fruit mixture ingredients to a boil in a large saucepan over high heat, reduce the heat to low and let the mixture simmer for 10–15 minutes, until it starts to thicken. Spoon the mixture into a 1 quart greased casserole dish.

In a large bowl combine all of the topping ingredients and mix until the oats are well moistened. Spread over the top of the fruit mixture. Cook for 20 minutes, reduce the heat to 350 degrees and continue to cook another 20–30 minutes until the fruit is bubbling and the oats are slightly browned.

Topping

> 8 tablespoons butter, softened
> 1 cup rolled (not instant) oats
> ¼ cup honey or agave nectar
> 1 teaspoon ground cinnamon

A note on healthy oatmeal: The coarser the better! If you are looking for the healthiest of oats, go with steel-cut or coarse cuts. That wimpy oatmeal that you can throw in the microwave for 30 seconds is neither healthy nor tasty. Keep it on the store shelf.

Famous People
with
Virgo South Node –
Pisces North Node

Naomi Campbell –

Naomi is such a perfectionist she likes to beat on cameras and scream when she doesn't get what she wants. She uses the fire of her Sagittarius Moon to act out a bit. It is also interesting that her South Node of Virgo is in the 8th house of personal power. She had a good deal of power in her previous lives and had people around her who had to jump to her demands of perfection. One very Virgo quote attributed to her is that she likes "fruit especially pineapple." Only a Virgo would have fruit as their favorite food. You would never catch a Leo saying that. Not when there are so many rich foods in which the king can indulge.

Charles Baudelaire–

"A healthy man can go without food for days, but not without poetry." The French poet was making a very Pisces North Node statement because Pisces doesn't care for things of the Earth – they are more concerned with the spiritual, the ethereal.

According to one of his chefs, Virgo Sun Michael Jackson's favorite foods were very Virgoan in nature with organic vegetable and fruit juices topping the list.

libra

Chapter 9

Ruled by Venus, Libra epitomizes the idea of sharing beautiful food with friends. This is the sign that loves to entertain others. Libra is all about the other person, even to the point of co-dependence. Libra does almost everything for others. Friends, companions and parties are right up the Libra alley. (I have Libra rising.) Libra vibrates to the 7th house. Traditionally, it was known as the "house of marriage," however, astrologers have now made that a bit broader and it is the house of all important, personal contractual relationships. It is the house where we get into the personal business of other people.

It is important for Libra to share with others. Being an Air Sign they aren't too excited about heavy or difficult-to-prepare meals and they like things that are balanced. After all they are symbolized by the scales.

Positive aspects of Libra include:
mediation skills, friendliness, being a great companion and a deep sense of caring for others.

Shadow aspects of Libra include:
co-dependence, indecisiveness, procrastination and a lack of self-awareness.

Foodie aspects of Libra include:
foods that can be shared, visually pleasing foods and a balanced menu.

Famous People with Libra Rising

Doris Day – She was and is America's sweetheart with a very Libran smile. I read a 1996 interview she gave to *OK Magazine* where the only food mentioned was that which she gave to her animals. "Anybody can feed them canned food. We don't want that. Today, they're having turkey loaves – ground turkey with eggs and whole wheat bread, lots of garlic, some onion, fresh tomatoes – and then we bake it. Then brown rice and vegetable soup made with chicken stock and noodles. For dessert, they have cookies made from oats and sunflower seeds with juice from the liver cooked for the cats." That is a very special person who applies Libran aesthetics to her pets.

Rock Hudson – Yes, he too was a beautiful, gentle creature and it is not coincidental that he and Doris were so compatible on screen and such good friends in real life. They shared a Libran sensibility. I found a recipe for a chicken paprika that is alleged to have been his favorite that calls for sherry, noodles and petite peas. Only someone ruled by Venus would ask for peas to be petite; nothing clunky for Libra.

Individual Smoked Salmon and Mushroom Frittatas

Frittatas aren't just for breakfast. When you make them in individual ramekins and serve with a tangy salsa, they make a great crowd-pleasing appetizer, perfect for the share-and-share alike Libran. Making one half mushroom and the other half salmon appeals to Libra's sense of balance.

It is a colossal pain to clean the cupcake pans after making these, even if you spray the heck out of them, so I make them with little cupcake liners or tins. They are cute, easy to eat from and you can change the cups with the season. Libra will love that.

Appetizer

12 disposable cupcake liners
1 tablespoon extra-virgin olive oil
10 ounces fresh medium mushrooms, sliced in half
¼ teaspoon kosher salt
1 dozen large eggs, lightly beaten
¼ teaspoon freshly ground black pepper
4 tablespoons fresh chives, chopped
½ cup Pecorino cheese, grated
6 ounces smoked salmon, cubed

Serves 6

For Salsa

1 tablespoon extra-virgin olive oil
3 red tomatoes, diced
1 small red onion, diced
2 jalapenos, diced
3 tomatillos, husk removed and diced
3 garlic cloves, diced
⅛ cup cilantro, chopped (parsley works if you are like me and hate cilantro)

Preheat the oven to 375 degrees: place the cupcake liners in a cupcake pan.

Heat the oil in a medium sauté pan over medium heat, add the mushrooms and salt and cook about 4 minutes until the mushrooms are lightly browned. Remove from heat to cool.

Divide the eggs, pepper, chives, and cheese into 2 medium bowls. In one of the bowls place the cooked mushrooms and in the other the salmon. Stir both mixtures until well blended.

Fill ½ of the cupcake liners with the mushroom mixture and then the other half with the salmon mixture.

Bake about 15 minutes until the muffins begin to puff up and brown.

While the frittatas are cooking, prepare the salsa. Combine all ingredients but the cilantro in a medium sauté pan over medium heat; cook for 10 minutes until the onion begins to brown and the mixture is no longer watery. Remove to a food processor and add the cilantro. Process it about 2–3 minutes until smooth.

Serve frittatas with salsa on the side.

Soup

A Duo of Roasted Butternut Squash and Apple Soups

I make a roasted butternut squash and apple soup, but thought it would be fun to split them up to make a sort of a yin/yang presentation as homage to the duality of this Air Sign that is always seeking balance.

Squash Soup

2 tablespoons extra-virgin olive oil
2 medium butternut squash
2 acorn squash
2 medium white onions
3 garlic cloves
3 teaspoons kosher salt
2 teaspoons cayenne pepper
2 teaspoons cinnamon
½ teaspoon cardamom
3 cups chicken or vegetable stock (see page 44)
1 cup milk

Serves 6 – 8

Apple Soup

1 tablespoon extra-virgin olive oil
10 medium red apples, seeded and cored
2 medium sweet potatoes*, quartered
1 medium white onion
4 cups chicken or vegetable stock
4 tablespoons maple syrup
½ teaspoon cayenne pepper
4 tablespoons fresh thyme
1 teaspoon kosher salt

Serves 6 – 8

Sage Topping

1 teaspoon extra-virgin olive oil
3 sage leaves

Preheat the oven to 400 degrees.

In a large roasting pan place the oil, squash, onions and garlic. (I hate cutting raw squash so I put them in whole. If you are stronger than I am you can quarter the squash, clean all seeds out, and then roast.) Bake about 45–70 minutes until all of the vegetables are fork tender. If you haven't already quartered and cleaned the squash, do so after they are cool to the touch.

Once the veggies are at room temperature, place them in a food processor with the spices and puree; slowly pour in the chicken stock and milk. If you have to work in batches, that is fine. You can either freeze or refrigerate for later use or place in a large saucepan and keep warm.

To make the apple soup, preheat the oven to 400 degrees. In a roasting pan place the oil, apples, potatoes and onion and bake about 30 minutes until all of the vegetables are fork tender.

Place the vegetables in a food processor. Puree while pouring in the stock and maple syrup. Season with the pepper, thyme and salt. You can either freeze or refrigerate for later use or place in a large saucepan and warm through.

To make the sage topping heat the olive oil in a small sauté pan over low heat. Add the sage leaves for about 2 minutes until just crisp. Remove to a dish covered with a paper towel. To serve to your favorite Libra, ladle half of the squash soup in half of the bowl and the apple in the other half. Sprinkle with the roasted pumpkin seeds (see page 90) and the fried sage leaves and serve hot.

A note on sweet potatoes: Don't refrigerate sweet potatoes until they are cooked. Store them in a cool place that is no more than 60 degrees and no colder than 35.

Jean Garofalo Porte's Pizza

Pizza is great for so many reasons but is especially for the ever-sharing Libra. And NO you don't put pineapple or ham or any of the other horrible toppings I have seen being tossed on the pies. Slice some good Italian sausage on top if you desire, add some mushroom slices if you must but that is IT. Do it all carefully and in symmetry. You don't want to offend the artistic Libran sensibility.

For Dough

> 2 cups warm (100 to 110 degrees) water
> 1 package dry yeast
> 2 cups all-purpose flour and extra for kneading
> 1 teaspoon kosher salt
> 2 tablespoons extra-virgin olive oil

For Topping

> 1 pound mozzarella cheese, cut into ½-inch slices
> 30 large fresh basil leaves

Makes 3 large pizzas

For the Sauce

> 1 teaspoon extra-virgin olive oil
> 3 garlic cloves, diced
> 3 teaspoons fresh oregano, minced
> 3 teaspoons fresh thyme, minced
> 2 28-ounce cans diced tomatoes
>   (I use the tomatoes I roast in the
>   summer – see page 21)
> 1 teaspoon kosher salt
> 1 teaspoon freshly ground black pepper
> 1 teaspoon red pepper flakes

Use a thermometer to test the water – too hot and you kill the yeast, too cold and the yeast sits there and giggles at you. In a large bowl combine the water and yeast. Let it sit a few minutes until the yeast froths. Add the flour and salt and combine totally. Roll out onto a floured surface and knead the dough until it is smooth and elastic.

Pour the oil in a clean, large bowl. Place the dough in the bowl; turning it over and over to be sure it is covered all over by the oil. Cover with a clean dish towel and place in a warm spot in the kitchen. Allow it to rest at least 1 hour – 2 is better.

A note on pizza: You don't need fancy pizza stones or any other equipment. A good 14-inch round pie pan does the job just as well.

At this point you can make the sauce. In a large soup pot over medium heat warm the olive oil and then sauté the garlic for 1 minute. Stir in the oregano and thyme and continue to sauté for another minute. Don't let the garlic burn. Stir in the tomatoes, salt and pepper and heat until the sauce begins to bubble. Reduce the heat and allow the sauce to simmer for about 1 hour.

Preheat the oven to 350 degrees.

To assemble the pizza, roll out the dough on a lightly floured surface until it is the size of your baking dish – again a 14-inch round is a great size – and about ¼ inch thick. Ladle a thin cover of sauce over the dough. The dough should be lightly covered but not drowning in sauce. Did you hear that, Taurus and Leo? There is no need to be a sauce glutton. Soggy is not sexy. If you must add sausage or mushrooms layer them on now in a single layer. Don't let me catch you adding any other nonsense to the top of that pizza.

Place the mozzarella cheese over top Don't load the cheese on... good Italian pizza is a balance of tastes – another reason the Libra will like it! Top with the basil leaves.

Veggies & Fruit

Mushy Peas

Libra rules the kidney area so we have to take care of Libra's kidneys! Peas are one of the many green veggies that are great for the kidneys. I fell in love with mushy peas in England – they are fun and delicious and Libra will love the little mint sprig on top!

    2 tablespoons extra-virgin olive oil
    1 medium bunch scallions, chopped
    ¾ pound frozen peas
    ½ stick salted butter, softened
    ¼ cup heavy cream
    1 teaspoon kosher salt
    1 teaspoon freshly ground black pepper
    ¼ cup fresh mint leaves

    Serves 6

Heat the oil in a medium sauté pan over low heat. Add the scallions and peas, cover and allow to steam for about 5 minutes. Transfer the mixture to a food processor, and pulse while adding the butter, cream, salt and pepper slowly. Continue to pulse it until smooth.

If you are not serving immediately, you can refrigerate up to 24 hours and reheat over a low heat. (Add a few tablespoons of milk or cream so it won't stick.) Just before serving place the mint leaves on top.

Sweet Potato Soufflé

This is a great potluck dish. Libra, with their hordes of friends, probably goes to lots of potluck dinners. This is a quick and elegant dish and very easy to transport.

    4 cups sweet potatoes, cooked and roughly chopped
    ¼ cup butter, softened
    ½ cup brown sugar
    ¼ cup milk
    3 eggs, beaten
    ¼ teaspoon kosher salt
    ¼ teaspoon pure vanilla extract

Topping

    ½ cup either halved pecans or walnuts, or raisins.
    ⅛ cup brown sugar
    ½ cup coconut
    2 tablespoons butter, softened

    Serves 8

(If it is holiday time add some cranberries. In winter, when citrus is plentiful, use orange segments.)

Preheat the oven to 425 degrees.

Spray the bottom and sides of a 10 inch baking dish, or 8 ramekins, with olive oil spray.

In a food processor pulse together all of the ingredients, except for the topping mix. Continue to pulse until the ingredients are mixed, then process until the mixture is very smooth. Turn it into the baking dish. Combine the topping ingredients until well mixed. Sprinkle over the top of the sweet potato mixture.

You can refrigerate the dish for up to 24 hours, or even freeze it and cook later.

Bake 30–45 minutes until the dish is bubbling.
Serve immediately.

A note on brown sugar: Yes it can be a big pain. I keep mine in the freezer and if it gets too hard I set it in a dish in the microwave with a small dish of water next to it. Nuke it for about 45 seconds and it should be nice and soft. If not, hit it for another 15 seconds.

A note on buying American- fish: I learned the hard way once when I didn't pay attention to the label and wound up with Chinese shrimp. Asian shrimp, tilapia and other fish farms are not regulated well, if at all. In fact, there is some evidence that they are from polluted waters and treated with chemicals. Try to buy your fish fresh from a local monger. If you can't do that, then at least read the labels on the packages. American may be a bit more expensive but in the long run it is better for everyone.

Meat & Fish

Easy New England Clam Bake

Clam bakes are a great way for Libra to share with friends; however, they can be intimidating. I know we all don't have room to go burying clams in the sand, so take the idea of a clam bake and make it work for you. I learned from my summers in Maine that most locals don't have the time or desire to do the traditional on-the-beach clam bake and so they hire out people to do it or scale things way down. Get a great big pot and cook everything on the stove; it works just as well.

I know that a lot of clam bake recipes demand that you add seaweed to the food. I never found seaweed to be much good for anything except to be annoying. If you feel you need seaweed, by all means add some with the corn. However, no New England ghosts will haunt you if you decide to leave it out.

3 pounds small red potatoes

3 large white onions, cut in half

10 garlic cloves, diced

4- 5 cups chicken stock, divided
(for homemade see page 44)

10 ears corn, cut in half

1 cup vermouth

Serves 8 – 10

4 pounds round clams, scrubbed

2 pounds mussels, cleaned and debearded

4 large lobster tails (or the whole lobster if you
are up for it.)

2 pounds unpeeled shrimp

1 stick butter, sliced into 3 pieces

10 lemons, cut in half

In a very large, deep pot layer the potatoes, onions and garlic. Pour in a cup of chicken stock, cover and cook over medium heat about 30 minutes, until the potatoes are just getting fork tender. Add the corn and cook another 10 minutes. Add the rest of the stock, the vermouth, clams and mussels (fish should be submerged in liquid) and cook for another 10–15 minutes; the clams and mussels should start to open. Add the lobster tails, shrimp and butter and cook for 10 more minutes.

When the shrimp are pink and the shells of the clams and mussels open, remove all of the food carefully into large bowls. Pour some of the sauce over the fish and serve with lemons and more butter for the corn.

Smorgasbord

Yes, that is right. What is better for a people person like a Libra than a good Scandinavian *smorgasbord*?

The original definition of the word is "sandwich table" but it has evolved into meaning a wide array of meats.

I think it would be fun for Libra to go back to an old-fashioned sandwich table they can share with friends with a few modern embellishments. First, go to a good food store and ravage the olive bar. You can place a variety of olives in little dishes among the sandwiches for aesthetics and nice nibbles. Then get some good heirloom tomatoes, a few assortments of good lettuce – I like Romaines and Bibbs – and then buy some good mustard (no runny yellow stuff) and mayonnaise. Lay all of them out on the table before you put out the sandwiches.

If you are the bread-making type, whip up your favorite good, hearty, grainy breads. If you are pressed for time, go to your favorite bakery and get three different types of whole grain, rye and pumpernickel breads. I have included my favorite pumpernickel recipe below. Once you make the sandwich breads, make up the sandwiches, distributing the meat equally among the different breads.

Set all of the food out and tell the Libra you invited a few of her many friends in to share the meal with her!

Chicken Pesto Sandwich

1 tablespoon extra-virgin olive oil
1 cup basil pesto (see pesto recipe on page 33)
4 boneless, skinless chicken breasts

2 teaspoons kosher salt
2 teaspoons freshly ground black pepper
8 slices Fontina cheese

Serves 8

Salt and pepper each side of the chicken breasts.

If you want to get a nice grill taste and weather permits, heat the grill (charcoal preferred) and cook the breasts over a low fire about 5 minutes on each side, until there is no pink in the middle.

If cooking inside, heat a tablespoon of olive oil in a medium sauté pan over medium heat and cook the breasts in the pan – again, until there is no pink in the middle – about 5 minutes on each side.

Remove the breasts from the heat and set aside until they are cool to the touch. Cube the chicken into about ½ inch cubes and mix with the pesto. Put the chicken on the bread and place a slice of cheese on top of the chicken.

If grilling, put the sandwiches back on the grill for 1–2 minutes until the cheese just starts to melt. You can also put the sandwiches under a low broiler for 1–2 minutes or you can put them back in the pan again and heat for 2–3 minutes on each side. Serve immediately.

A note on freezing pesto: Do it! It is great to open in the dark of winter and get hit with the wonderful smell of basil!

Mediterranean Salad Sandwich

This is fun and you don't have to assemble it – just put all of the pieces on the table and let people build their own.

3 medium eggplants, sliced into ¼-inch pieces
4 large red peppers, seeded, cored and
    sliced into 1 inch long pieces
2 teaspoons kosher salt
2 teaspoons freshly ground black pepper

Serves 8

2-3 tablespoons extra-virgin olive oil
3 Portobello mushrooms, sliced
    into 1-inch-long pieces
2 garlic cloves, roughly chopped
¼ cup pine nuts

Preheat the oven to 250 degrees.

Sprinkle the salt and pepper over the eggplants and peppers. Place about 2 tablespoons of the olive oil in a shallow roasting pan and slowly roast the eggplants and peppers for 90 minutes, until they are soft but not burned. Halfway through the roasting process add the mushrooms and garlic to the other vegetables. Be sure to mix them well so they are coated with the olive oil and add more oil if the mixture is dry.

Thirty minutes before the vegetables are done, place the pine nuts in another roasting pan that has been sprayed with cooking oil and put in the oven.

Remove the vegetables and serve in one dish and the pine nuts in another on your *smorgasbord* table.

Cobb Sandwich

This is based on the famous Cobb salad.

4 chicken breasts
3 teaspoons kosher salt
2 teaspoons freshly ground black pepper
3 teaspoons fresh tarragon, minced

serves 8

14 slices apple smoked bacon
¾ cup of your favorite blue cheese dressing
3 hardboiled eggs, cooled and diced
3 ripe avocados, sliced

Preheat the oven to 375 degrees.

Spray a roasting pan with oil spray. Season the chicken breasts with salt, pepper and tarragon and cook about 25 minutes, turning at least once until both sides are nicely browned. Remove from the oven and once cooled to the touch slice into 1-inch-long pieces.

Cook the bacon over medium heat in a medium sauté pan until crisp. Remove to paper towels off of the stove to cool.

Spread the blue cheese dressing on both sides of the pumpernickel bread (see page 167) and layer the chicken, eggs, avocados and bacon into the sandwich and serve immediately

A note on avocados: If you cut one in half and it is too unripe to use, sprinkle the flesh with lemon juice, place the two halves together again, wrap with plastic wrap and put in the refrigerator. Check them every half hour until they are ripe enough to use.

Pumpernickel Bread

½ tablespoon active dry yeast

½ cup molasses

4 teaspoons kosher salt

2 tablespoons vegetable oil

2 tablespoons caraway seeds

3 tablespoons unsweetened cocoa powder

2 ¾ cups rye flour

3 cups bread flour

⅛ cup cornmeal

Makes 2 rounds

Stir together the yeast and 1½ cups of warm water in a medium bowl until yeast is dissolved. Then add the molasses, salt, oil, caraway seeds, cocoa powder and rye flour. This is where you need the patience of the Earth Signs, because you then have to slowly add in 2 cups of the regular flour, mix well and turn out to a floured bread board. Knead the dough for 5–8 minutes. If it is still sticky, knead in more flour about ⅛ cup at a time. Keep kneading and adding until the bread is not sticky.

Spray a medium bowl with cooking spray. Place the dough in the bowl and flip it around until it is lightly greased on all sides. Cover with a clean dish towel, place in a warm spot and let it rise for an hour or two, until it is doubled in size.

Now the Fire Signs can kick in, because you have to punch it down. Grease the bowl again, place the dough back in, move it around in the bowl, cover and let rise again for another hour or two. When it is doubled in size again, punch it down. Turn the dough out onto the floured board again and knead for a few minutes.

Cut the dough in half and form 2 small rounds. Grease a baking sheet with oil spray and sprinkle with the cornmeal. Place the dough rounds on the sheet, cover and let it rise for another hour.

Preheat the oven to 375 degrees.

Bake the rounds for 35 minutes or until you lightly tap the bottoms and they sound hollow. Cool on a wire rack. You can freeze the rounds at this point if you have to.

To Their Health

Orange Cranberry Compote

Libra rules the kidneys and urinary tract area. Cranberries are very good at keeping this area in good shape. I often make this compote at Thanksgiving but it is good anytime you have fish or poultry. Often the ones you buy in the store are full of sugar – not a good thing.

1 12-ounce bag cranberries
2 tablespoons orange zest, grated
1 tablespoon lemon zest, grated
1 cup fresh orange juice
1 teaspoon pure vanilla extract
¼ cup granulated sugar

Serves 8

Place all of the ingredients in a large saucepan and heat over medium heat. Stir often to melt the sugar and incorporate all of the ingredients. Cook for about 10 minutes after the cranberries have stopped popping, stirring often.

Remove from heat and cool. You can serve cold or at room temperature and this freezes very well.

Opposites Attract: Stretching Your Libra South Node

Libras are moving to Aries – literally, it is a movement from "we" to "me." Librans have to learn the art of being more self- centered, in a good way, and being less co-dependent. They need to act without the chorus of voices in their heads wondering if what they are doing is acceptable to their friends. The idea of cooking for one is not something that is remotely easy for a Libran. I knew a Libra-influenced chef who would cook fantastic meals for friends and when alone resorted to pre-packed, microwave "food." This is a dish that will help Libra remember that they are the most important person in the universe!

Lobster for One

1 teaspoon butter, softened
3 teaspoons panko
1 asparagus spear, cooked and diced
Meat from 1 shelled lobster tail, cubed
1 hardboiled egg, chopped
2 teaspoons fresh lemon juice
2 teaspoons fresh chives, diced
⅛ cup light cream

Serves ONE

Preheat the oven to 350 degrees.

Grease the inside of an individual gratin dish with the butter. Sprinkle the panko over the butter, being sure to cover the inside of the dish. Lay the asparagus in a single line on the bottom of the gratin dish. In a large bowl mix the lobster meat, egg, lemon juice, chives and cream. Pour over the asparagus.

Bake about 15 minutes, until lobster is just opaque. Serve immediately.

Dessert

Chocolate Mousse Parfait

Venus was called Aphrodite when the Greeks were in power. Chocolate was always associated with this lady because of its qualities as an aphrodisiac. We can't end the Libra section without sending them off with a scrumptious chocolate dessert. Libra will like the balance of chocolate and raspberry. They love all things in balance and so often don't find it in this harsh world.

Parts of this dish have to cool for at least four hours; overnight is better, so plan accordingly.

8 ounces semisweet chocolate, coarsely chopped
3 large egg yolks
1 tablespoon coffee
1 cup heavy cream
1 pint fresh raspberries, (save some for decoration)

Serves 6

1 teaspoon orange liqueur
1 cup seedless raspberry jam
1 teaspoon butter
5 graham crackers, crumbled
½ teaspoon cinnamon

Place the chocolate on the top of a double boiler over simmering water (medium heat.) Stir occasionally until the chocolate has melted. Stir in the egg yolks and coffee, mixing well. Remove from the heat and allow to cool.

Beat the cream in a medium bowl until it comes to soft peaks. Fold almost all but 2 tablespoons of the cream into the coffee/chocolate mixture. Cover and refrigerate for at least 4 hours or overnight.

Combine the raspberries, 1 cup of water, liqueur and jam in a medium saucepan over medium heat. Cook for about 5 minutes, smashing the raspberries gently and mixing all of the ingredients together. Place them into a food processor and pulse for a few minutes until smooth. Refrigerate at least 4 hours or overnight.

Remove the mousse from the refrigerator and spoon ½ of it into pretty parfait glasses or martini glasses. Spoon ½ inch of raspberry sauce on top of the mousse and then gently spread it. Spoon the rest of the mousse mixture over the raspberry. Return parfaits to the refrigerator.

Melt the butter in a small sauté pan over low heat, add the graham crackers and cinnamon and mix well. Cook about 1 minute. Remove from the heat and cool.

Sprinkle the graham crackers over the top of the mousse. Serve each parfait with a raspberry and dollop of the remaining whipped cream.

Famous People with
Libra South Node – Aries North Node

Meryl Streep –

The best actress of our generation or perhaps any, she uses her Libra artistry to portray amazing characters. Venus has helped her relationship-wise as she and her husband have had a long marriage and raised four kids who have stayed out of the media circus. A native of my home state, New Jersey, she gave an interview recently where she extolled the virtues of the Jersey tomato. She is right. No place does pizza, pasta and tomatoes better than New Jersey. However, diplomatically, like all good Libras, she claims she doesn't have a favorite food.

Richard Gere –

Venus sure did shine on his pretty face didn't she? He owns a restaurant in a rural setting in a building that he and his wife have restored and which includes a yoga studio. If that isn't Libra balance I don't know what is.

North Node in Libra Tina Turner exhibits Libran indecisiveness
when it comes to her food favorites. She claims that her food loves
have moved from Soul food, to Thai to Italian!

175

scorpio

Chapter 10

 I know Scorpio is all about pot boiling, wild hanging from the chandeliers sex, right? Please. Can we put away the stereotypes? Scorpio is really all about power – the power to change – the power to soar to the heights of spiritual awareness or the power to plumb the lowest depths of depravity. No one with Scorpio prominently placed in their charts leaves this Earth the same person they were when they were born. Now I know you can say – well doesn't everyone change? Not really. Think about it. Don't you know people who are just the same person they were as kids? Yeah, we all know a lot. But not Scorpio – for better or worse, they will be different as they reach the exit sign.

Speaking of exit, Scorpio vibrates to the 8th house, the traditional house of death and dying, the ultimate transformation. The 8th is where we connect with that power to transform ourselves. Pluto, the cold, distant planet*, is the ruler of Scorpio. Pluto forces long term change and is a "generational" planet, that is, it is so slow that it forces change for at least a generation. (Those of us born during the baby boom are all Pluto in Leo babies. That is why we caused so much trouble and insisted that everyone look at and pay attention to us! Now Pluto is in Capricorn, bringing change to governments and structures of authority.)

Scorpios also like to ferret out secrets – your secrets, not theirs – never theirs! They like drama and mysteries and the unknown. Digging deep through the layers to find what makes things and people tick is their passion. So we will indulge all of their little idiosyncrasies with our collection of meals!

Positive aspects of Scorpio include:
loyalty, passion, resourcefulness and courage.

Shadow aspects of Scorpio include:
vengeance, deception and excessive secretiveness.

Foodie aspects of Scorpio include:
food with drama, flair and a hint of surprise.

♈ ♉ ♊ ♋ ♌ ♍ ♎ ♏ ♐ ♑ ♒ ♓

Famous People with Scorpio Rising

Jacqueline Kennedy Onassis – You can often tell a Scorpio by their eyeglasses. Because they like to be secretive they often hide behind them. Jacqueline made her over-sized sun glasses famous. They were her shield against intrusions into privacy. (Although with her Leo Sun I will also contend that she liked publicity but because of her Scorpio power-control thing it had to be on her terms.) In her book *Cooking for Madam: Recipes and Reminiscences from the Home of Jacqueline Kennedy Onassis,* Marta Sgubin, who worked for her for years, mentioned that one of her favorite dishes was truffle soup topped with phyllo dough. Who could resist divulging their deepest secrets when being presented this wonderful soup!

Grace Kelly – She was actually a double Scorpio – Scorpio Sun and Scorpio rising. Princess Grace was the epitome of the icy seductress. Behind closed doors she was quite sexually "active", but she never pierced that secretive Scorpio veil when in public. When she attended a lunch at the Kennedy White House, her fellow Scorpio rising, Jacqueline Kennedy, served her Strawberries Romanoff and Spring Lamb Á La Broche Aux Primeurs. That is Scorpio dramatic talk for strawberries and cream and a lamb on a spit with spring veggies. Yes, I know that the White House fancies up the language on these things, but this is that bit of extra dramatic Scorpio talk.

*Yes, it may be an asteroid, may be a minor planet or may be back as a big planet. The debate rages. However, it is very important to karmic Astrology because it rules big, deep changes which are why we are all here in the first place.

Appetizer

Chicken (or Pork) Lettuce Wraps

Lettuce wraps are often served with iceberg lettuce. As a child of the '50s and '60s I have had my fill of iceberg lettuce and I can't understand all of the recent excitement over the little green pieces of cardboard. I prefer sweet delicate Bibb; it is tastier and folds nicer to make a lovely packet for your Scorpio, who loves things that are hidden. As I said, secrets are their thing.

32 whole Bibb lettuce leaves
4 teaspoons extra-virgin olive oil, divided
2 large white onions, diced
1 teaspoon sugar
2 garlic cloves, minced
2 pounds ground chicken or pork

1 tablespoon soy sauce
½ cup good hoisin sauce
2 tablespoons red wine vinegar
1 cup pine nuts, finely chopped
16 ounces water chestnuts (If you get canned
   be sure to drain), finely chopped

Serves 8

Gently pull the Bibb lettuce leaves off of the head. Wash them and then dry by gently patting between paper towels. Set aside.

In a large sauté pan over low heat, warm 3 teaspoons of the oil, add the onions and sugar and caramelize slowly, 25-30 minutes. If you are a patient Earth Sign take you time. The more caramelized the yummier the onions become. Add the garlic and cook another 5 minutes. Do not burn the garlic. Remove the garlic and onions and set aside to cool in a large bowl.

In the same sauté pan add the meat. (You may have to add a little more oil if it is dry.) Cook over medium heat, breaking the meat up, for about 10 minutes until it is browned. Remove to the same bowl as the onions and garlic. Add the soy and hoisin sauces, and vinegar and stir well.

Add the other teaspoon of oil to the sauté pan and add the pine nuts. Cook about 1 minute until lightly browned. Add the water chestnuts and sauté for 2 more minutes.

Immediately before serving, return the meat mixture to the sauté pan and heat all of the ingredients while mixing well.

While the meat is heating, lay out the lettuce leaves on a flat service. Scoop about 2 tablespoons of meat mixture into the center of each leaf. Roll the leaves over and fold the sides toward the center to make little packets. Serve immediately – you don't want wilted lettuce.

♈ ♉ ♊ ♋ ♌ ♍ ♎ ♏ ♐ ♑ ♒ ♓

Soup

Creamy Carrot Ginger Soup

Carrots are a power food and the perfect pick-me-up for a Scorpio needing a little charge. Being such intense little creatures, they need to recharge often. The ginger gives this soup a nice warming zing that appeals to the Scorpio's need for a bite. If your Scorpio has a lot of Virgo or Cancer in their chart, they might want something healthier so feel free to use veggie stock and replace the cream with plain Greek yogurt.

2 tablespoons extra-virgin olive oil
3 garlic cloves, minced
1 cup white onions, chopped
½ teaspoon kosher salt
⅛ cup fresh ginger, minced
1 pound carrots, peeled and roughly chopped
1 medium russet potato, peeled and roughly chopped

4-6 cups chicken stock (see page 44)
½ teaspoon freshly ground black pepper
2 cup heavy cream or plain yogurt
2 teaspoons fresh thyme, diced
a few sprigs of parsley, for garnish

Serves 8

In a large soup pot over low heat, add the olive oil and garlic. Cook about 1 minute until garlic is just starting to lightly brown. Do not burn. Remove to a side dish off of the heat. Add the onions and salt to the pot. Stirring occasionally, cook the onions 20–30 minutes until nicely browned. (You can actually slow cook onions for up to an hour to get even greater carmelization.)

Increase the heat to medium. Add the ginger, carrots, potato and 4 cups of the stock. Return the garlic to the pot and stir all ingredients well. Add the pepper and more salt if needed. Cover and cook about 20 minutes until the carrots and potatoes are just turning soft.

Remove the soup from the heat and cool a bit. Remember, you don't want to blend boiling hot soup it can be dangerous. If you have an immersion blender, insert it into the pot and blend while pouring all but ¼ cup of the cream into the pot. If you do not have an immersion blender then use your food processor to blend the soup. Add the thyme and stir well.

Return the soup to the heat to warm. Just before serving sprinkle the parsley and remaining cream on top.
Serve immediately.

A note on ginger: Ginger freezes well. Keep a hunk in your freezer and grate some off as needed.

Pasta

Pasta Puttanesca

This is one of my favorite pastas (I am a Scorpio Sun after all) and a tongue in cheek wink to the so called sexual prowess of this sign. Among the many origins accredited to this pasta is that it was the specialty of the ladies of the evening in Italy because it was fast to make and hot and spicy like them.

4 tablespoons extra-virgin olive oil, divided

5 garlic cloves, minced

5 teaspoons kosher salt, divided

½ teaspoon red pepper flakes

1 teaspoon fresh oregano, diced

1 cup diced tomatoes,
   (or my roasted tomatoes. See page 21)

1 cup pitted Kalamata olives

¼ cup capers

5 anchovy fillets (you can leave them
   out if they gross you out!)

¼ cup white wine

2 pounds linguini or other thin spaghetti
   although I find angel hair nothing but annoying

3 teaspoons fresh flat-leaf Italian parsley,
   roughly chopped

1 cup fresh basil leaves, gently torn in half

¼ cup Parmigiano-Reggiano cheese, grated

Serves 8

In a large sauté pan over medium heat add 3 tablespoons of the olive oil, garlic and 2 teaspoons of salt. Sauté until the garlic is lightly browned – about 1 minute. Do not burn the garlic. Add the red pepper flakes, oregano and tomatoes, stirring well. Cook another 5 minutes then add the olives, capers, anchovies and wine. Reduce the heat to low and simmer about 20 minutes until all of the flavors are incorporated and most of the liquid is evaporated.

Fill a large soup pot with about 5 quarts of water, the rest of the olive oil and the remaining salt. Cover and bring to a boil. Add the pasta and cook about 7–8 minutes until *al dente*. Drain immediately. Pour the pasta and parsley into the tomato sauce and toss well. Turn into a large serving bowl and place the basil leaves over top. Serve immediately with your best Parmigiano sprinkled on top.

Veggies & Fruit

Stuffed Roasted Beets

Anyone can stuff a mushroom or a tomato but Scorpio likes to be different – so how about a stuffed beet? Scorpios love to get inside things and find the secrets, so give them some secret sausage! Red is also a good Scorpio color.

16 large fresh beets
   (You can do 8 large beets but I hate having
   one veggie per person – being Italian I am of
   the "make more and give leftovers" school.)
1 teaspoon extra-virgin olive oil
3 garlic cloves, diced
16 ounces sausage meat – if you can't find loose
   sausage then take some out of the casings

Serves 8

1 cup Gruyere cheese, shredded
1 cup Fontina cheese, shredded
¼ cup ricotta cheese
1 teaspoon kosher salt
1 teaspoon freshly ground black pepper
3 tablespoons fresh flat-leaf Italian parsley, minced

Cut the roots and greens off of the beets – make sure the bottoms are flat so they stand easily. (Save the beet greens – see note on beets*.) Place the beets into a large saucepan and cover with water. Bring to a boil over high heat, then reduce heat to medium and let them gently cook for about 20–30 minutes. They are done when you can pierce them with a fork easily. (Be gentle, Fire Signs, each beet has to hold a stuffing so you don't want to stab them to death.) Drain, and place in a large bowl and allow to cool.

In a medium skillet heat the olive oil over medium heat, add the garlic and sauté about 2 minutes – until it starts to turn light brown. Remove to a small bowl to cool. Add the sausage to the pan, and cook thoroughly until browned, – about 10 minutes. Break the sausage up into small pieces so it fits into the beets easily. Turn off the heat and stir in the garlic.

Scoop out the inside of the beets using a melon baller or spoon, leaving about ¼-inch on the sides and bottom. Set the hollowed beet cups aside.

A note on beets: Always buy fresh. The canned ones don't taste – well, like much of anything. Chop off the beet greens, slice them up and toss into a sauté pan with some heated olive oil. Add some garlic, salt and pepper and cook them for a minute or two over medium heat. They are tasty and healthy. You can line the dish with the beet greens before you place the beets down if you want to use them in this dish.

Pulse the remaining chunks of beets in a food processor until very fine and place in a large bowl. Mix in the cheeses, salt and pepper until well combined. Stir in the sausage mixture. Gently fill each beet cup with some of the filling. Place filled beets in a shallow baking dish that has been lined with a sheet of aluminum foil. (This helps clean-up.)

Place under a low boiler for 3–5 minutes until the mixture begins to bubble.

Sprinkle with the parsley and serve immediately.

Zucchini Crepes

I came to this one in a roundabout way. Scorpios love a good mystery story. The world's "greatest detective" was Hercule Poirot who in one book retired to grow vegetable marrow – an English cousin to the zucchini. So I am using the zucchini to make a crepe and hide some yummy roasted tomatoes inside.

¾ cup zucchini, grated
1 cup all-purpose flour *
5 tablespoons butter, melted, divided
1¼ cups milk
2 eggs, beaten

¾ teaspoon kosher salt
2 teaspoons fresh thyme, chopped
2 teaspoons fresh oregano, chopped
2 cups roasted tomatoes (see page 21)
¼ cup good tomato sauce (see page 24)

Serves 8

Drain the zucchini in a colander for 30 minutes after grating it to get any excess water out.

In a large bowl slowly combine the flour, 1 tablespoon butter, milk eggs, and salt mixing thoroughly. The batter should have no lumps. You can mix in a blender or use an immersion blender if you prefer. Refrigerate the batter for at least 30 minutes.

Remove the batter from the refrigerator and stir in the zucchini, thyme and oregano.

To make the crepes, heat a crepe pan over medium heat and brush it with melted butter. With a small ice cream scooper place 2 teaspoons of the crepe batter in the pan and tilt it around so you have a thin layer on the bottom of the pan. The crepes should be almost paper-thin. Yes, Air Signs, you need to be careful but Virgos, no need to measure them to perfection! Cook for about 1 minute until the edges start to turn brown and the center is no longer wet. Remove the crepes to a cooling rack.

Continue until all of the batter is gone.

When the crepes are cool to the touch spread about 2 tablespoons of the roasted tomatoes down the center and then fold into thirds. Place fold side down onto a greased baking dish. Cover with a thin layer of the tomato sauce.

When ready to serve, reheat the crepes in a 300 degree oven for 15 – 20 minutes. Serve immediately.

*You can use whole wheat baking flour or gluten free flour – just add ⅛ cup more milk.

A note on crepes: You can make crepes well in advance. Just stack them up with a sheet of waxed paper between each, wrap well in a plastic bag and freeze. They are a great rainy afternoon project that you can pull out when in a hurry.

Meat & Fish

Negamaki Beef

Negamaki Beef is one of those fun little dishes that holds a secret inside. They are also small enough that you can eat them even in bed. Oh yes, Scorpios love to do everything – and I mean everything – in bed. They would prefer never to leave bed if they could!

1 teaspoon extra-virgin olive oil
1 teaspoon kosher salt
1 teaspoon freshly ground black pepper
24 thin asparagus stalks (or 12 larger stalks cut in half)

1 medium bunch of scallions
½ cup soy or hoisin sauce
1 ½ pounds beef tenderloin

Serves 6

Preheat the oven to 500 degrees.

A note on veggie stock: Use the chicken stock recipe on page 44 and just replace the chicken with veggies. While you can use things such as broccoli and asparagus stalks – and I do – you can also make stock with fresh vegetables. Like with the chicken stock, if you can take a little time to roast the veggies with some garlic and onions and some extra-virgin olive oil for about 50 minutes before you boil them, it adds more flavor.

Hold the asparagus in both hands and snap them quickly. Where they break is where they start to become hard. Use only the top soft portion of the asparagus. Either compost the bottoms or use later for a vegetable stock.*

Spread the oil on the bottom of a roasting dish. Lay the asparagus in a single layer in the dish and season with salt and pepper. Cook 8–10 minutes until the asparagus is just fork tender.

Cut the scallions into thin strips.

Slice the beef tenderloin into ¼ inch slices. Marinate the tenderloin pieces in the soy or hoisin sauce for about 30 minutes in the refrigerator.

Open each piece of tenderloin and place on a clean, flat surface. Place 1 slice of scallion and 2 pieces of asparagus length-wise in each piece of tenderloin so that they hang over the sides. Roll the tenderloin slices and place in a medium broiler cut side down. Cook 1 minute per side.

Broil 3–5 minutes until lightly charred. Serve immediately.

Mom's Beef Liver

Okay, I am going out on a limb with liver, but my Mom made the best liver. Liver is energy food and Scorpios need a great deal of energy to do all of that transformation! Trust me! No, we didn't have organic beef liver when I was a kid, but our meat wasn't pumped up with antibiotics and steroids then either. If you want to make the liver look less like liver slice it into strips before serving.

½ pound bacon
4 large white onions, diced
2 teaspoons kosher salt
2 tablespoons flour

Serves 8

3 teaspoons freshly ground black pepper
8 pieces of organic beef liver
½ cup white wine
⅛ cup fresh flat-leaf Italian parsley, chopped

In an electric flying pan cook the bacon over medium heat until crispy but not burnt. Remove the bacon and drain all but 5 tablespoons of the oil. Add the onions and salt to the frying pan and cook slowly over low heat for 20–30 minutes until they are lightly browned and caramelized. Stir in the flour and pepper, mix well so there are no lumps in the flour. Add the liver, bacon and wine and cook over medium heat 20–25 minutes. Stir in the parsley before serving.

A note on organics: In this case I would insist on using organic because liver just needs to be organic because of its nature. However, it is always good to buy organic, hormone- and antibiotic-free meat. Yes, you pay a bit more now but it really could help you save on medicines and doctors later.

To Their Health

Scorpios can be intense little creatures especially if they get into that possessive, revenge mode that they do so well. Since they are water creatures, I am going to give them a relaxing "prescription" from the sea. Shrimp is a great source of tryptophan and selenium, both essential to staying calm. Risotto is a very calming comfort food so the combination of the two makes for a great meal for your stressed out Scorp. Because they have hypnotic eyes to watch the risotto they will be sure that it doesn't burn. This is also a good dish for Scorpio to make as it can be very Zen and calming. Now if you can get an Aquarian or Libran out of the atmosphere and into risotto-making you will be doing really well.

Shrimp and Asparagus Risotto

4 tablespoons butter
2 cups Arborio rice
2 garlic cloves, minced, divided
½ teaspoon kosher salt
¼ teaspoon freshly ground black pepper
¼ cup white wine
6 cups fish stock, divided

Serves 8

1 large bunch asparagus, trimmed and
    cut into 2 inch pieces
⅛ cup extra-virgin olive oil
¾ pounds medium shrimp, peeled and deveined
1 cup Parmigiano-Reggiano cheese, grated
½ cup light cream
1 lemon, sliced

Preheat the oven to 350 degrees and butter a 12-inch baking dish.

Heat a medium sauté pan over medium heat, add the butter and when it is just melted add the Arborio rice and cook, stirring frequently, until the rice is well-coated and fragrant – about 1–2 minutes. Add all but 1 teaspoon of the garlic, and salt and pepper and cook, stirring – about 1 minute. Add the wine and cook another 2 minutes then add 2 cups of the fish stock.

Cook, stirring often until the stock has been absorbed. Continue to cook, adding more stock ½ cup at a time as it is absorbed, until the rice is *al dente*. Risotto has to be fed slowly – this will take about 18 minutes. If you use all of the stock before the rice is *al dente* add a bit of hot water as needed. Remove the rice from the heat.

Heat ½ cup of water in a medium saucepan over medium heat. Add the asparagus and blanch for about 2 minutes. Remove from heat, drain, place in a small bowl filled with ice to stop the cooking process.

Heat the olive oil in a large skillet until very hot. Add the shrimp and remaining garlic and cook until shrimp are lightly golden on both sides, 1–2 minutes. Remove to a small bowl and set aside.

Layer half of the reserved rice mixture in the prepared baking dish and sprinkle with half of the cheese. Top with the shrimp and garlic and asparagus, pressing down lightly to compress mixture. Add the remaining risotto and smooth the top with the back of a spoon. Top with the remaining cheese. Pour the cream over the mixture.

Bake 30 minutes until the mixture is set. Cool slightly and decorate with lemon slices before serving.

A note on fish and cheese: I know the thinking is that you never mix fish and cheese. I don't know about that but I do know that my Italian grandparents used to pile grated cheese on their shrimp scampi and pasta. If you are a prim and proper Virgo type or a stickler for doing what is expected, like Capricorn, then leave it out. I don't mind the cheese on this dish so maybe I am just a hopeless peasant.

Opposites Attract:
Stretching Your Scorpio South Node

Scorpios are moving toward Taurus, away from the powerful spiritual realm and toward getting their feet on the ground and enjoying being on Earth. Taurus loves all things earthy, tactile and even gluttonous. It would do Scorpio good to sit down with a good, fun gooey bowl of cheesy earthy French Onion Soup.

French Onion Soup

½ stick butter
3 ½ pounds yellow onions, sliced ¼-inch thick
4 leeks, green tops and roots removed,
    sliced ¼ inch thick
1 cup sherry
2 cups white wine
8 cups beef stock

Serves 8

½ teaspoon freshly ground black pepper
1 medium French baguette, slightly stale
2 tablespoons extra-virgin olive oil
½ cup Gruyere cheese, grated
½ cup Parmigiano-Reggiano cheese, grated

Preheat the oven to 350 degrees.

In a large soup pan over low heat melt the butter. Add the onions and leeks and sauté slowly about 35- 40 minutes, until the onions are a golden brown color. Raise the heat to medium and deglaze the pan with the sherry. Add the wine and simmer about 20 minutes, until the liquid is reduced to half its original volume. Add the beef stock and pepper. Bring to a boil, then reduce the heat to low and simmer for 30 minutes.

While the soup is cooking slice the baguette into ¼ inch rounds. Brush with olive oil, place on a flat sheet in single row. Bake for about 15 minutes until they are slightly brown.

Ladle the soup into oven-proof bowls, place 1 slice of bread in each bowl, and then cover the top of the soup with the cheeses. Place the bowls on a baking sheet and then under the broiler 1–2 minutes until the cheese starts to brown and bubble. Serve immediately – warn your guests that the dishes are hot!

Dessert

Calabeza En Tacha

This is a traditional dessert for the Mexican Day of the Dead celebrations. Scorpios are big on dramatic endings, so what better way to end their section?

1 4-5 pound pumpkin, seeded and cut into 3 inch slices*
8 cinnamon sticks
3 tablespoons sugar
7 whole cloves
Juice of 1 large orange
Juice of 1 medium lemon

Serves 6 – 8

In a large saucepan over medium heat combine 4 cups of water with the cinnamon, sugar, cloves, orange and lemon juices. Bring to a boil, stirring until the sugar is completely dissolved. Reduce the heat to low and carefully add the pumpkin pieces in layers.

Cover and simmer about 2 hours. The pulp should be soft and look glazed.

Cool the mixture – you can even refrigerate and serve this cold. I prefer room temperature or a bit warm with the sauce spooned over the pumpkin.

*Yes, you can cook it in advance as I have mentioned before and then slice and cut it. This pumpkin should take about 35 minutes in a 325 degree oven. If you cut the pumpkin before you make the dish you should only simmer the pumpkin for about an hour. If pumpkin is out of season use acorn squash.

Famous People with
Scorpio South Node – Taurus North Node

Mother Theresa –

Whether or not you agree with all she did, Mother Theresa is a great example of someone taking the best of her spiritual Scorpio South Node and applying it in a very Taurus way – touching those considered untouchable with hands-on care to provide food and comfort.

Kurt Cobain –

Here we have someone who stubbornly stayed in his Scorpio South Node of drama, and a fascination with the spiritual and death over life. I read that he once said his favorite food was "rice and water" – oh how dramatic, oh how Scorpio.

North Node in Scorpio Ludwig Beethoven apparently was very "into" the Scorpio love of hidden things. His favorite foods were stews, and macaroni hidden under piles of cheese – sort of an early version of mac-and-cheese

sagittarius

Chapter 11

Who is Sagittarius the Archer? Well he shoots his arrow into the air and searches the world for truth – his truth – actually his spiritual truth. Sagittarius is obsessed with finding and contextualizing the truth. Never ask a Sagittarian if you look fat in that dress because he will tell you – in spades. For Sag. it is all about what they know and they just know they know the truth!

Many people with Sagittarius rising are athletic, love to experience life and love to travel. They want to soak up other cultures and other religions to find out what they believe. Someone with Sagittarius on the 9th house cusp – the house that Sagittarius vibrates to will be on the go a lot and have important interactions with people from foreign cultures. The big, expansive planet Jupiter leads Sagittarius around the Zodiac, so they are all about getting out and expanding their knowledge and depth. A Fire Sign, Sagittarius likes variety and a wee bit of spice.

One thing people with a lot of Sagittarius or Jupiter in their 1st house have to watch for is expansion of body. Remember the 1st house is how we project our physicality and sometimes Jupiter can keep people in a constant battle of the bulge.

Positive aspects of Sagittarius include:
honesty, inquisitiveness, spiritual searching and a love of travel.

Shadow aspects of Sagittarius include:
overindulgence, risk taking and self-righteousness and being highly opinionated.

Foodie aspects of Sagittarius include:
adventurous foods, those with a foreign flair and a wide variety of foods.

Famous People with Sagittarius Rising

Princess Diana – She apparently became so concerned with her weight issues that she became bulimic. Diana also exhibited Sagittarius' athletic ability and spirituality as evidenced by her caring for people who were in need.

Marlon Brando – Well, I did say the shadow of Sagittarius was overindulgence, didn't I?

Appetizer

Tomato, Watermelon and Goat Cheese Salad

Start off your Sagittarius with something low fat – it helps keep the weight off. Since they are ruled by Jupiter, the ever-expansive planet, that is sometimes a bit of an issue with them. Although mascarpone isn't too caloric, you can always use a light cream cheese in its place to lower the calories even more.

5 ounces goat cheese

2 tablespoons mascarpone cheese

Serves 6

6 heirloom or beefsteak tomatoes, diced

3 cups watermelon, diced

10 fresh basil leaves

Cream the goat cheese and mascarpone together until they are smooth. Pour the cheeses into a medium size serving bowl. Place the tomatoes and watermelon on top and then add the basil leaves. Serve immediately.

A note on heirloom tomatoes: We are oh so pretentious about foods these days. Heirloom tomatoes are basically grown from seeds that have been passed down from generations of growers. They can be tastier than regular tomatoes but so many are commercially grown that unless you are buying from a farmer or CSA I don't think they are worth the extra money. If you can't get true heirlooms get beefsteaks.

Avgolemono or Greek Lemon Soup

I first had this soup in a little hole-in-the-wall restaurant in Baltimore and fell in love with the creamy texture. This soup done badly is like sucking on a sour lemon ball, so watch your hand when you are adding the lemon. It will remind your Jupiter baby to book that Greek cruise they always wanted to take.

8 cups chicken stock (to make your own see page 44)
1 cup rice or orzo pasta – you can use brown rice if you prefer
2 eggs
½ cup fresh lemon juice
2 teaspoons kosher salt
2 teaspoons freshly ground black pepper

Serves 6

In a large soup pot over medium heat bring the stock to a boil. Add the rice and lower the heat to cook slowly, stirring often, until the rice is cooked. If using a long grain or brown rice this could take up to 20 minutes. Orzo will cook in 5–10 minutes. Remove ½ cup of the stock into a small bowl and set aside to cool for about 15–20 minutes.

Beat the eggs well in a medium bowl. Slowly pour ¼ cup of stock into the eggs stirring constantly. Go slowly and beat a lot so the eggs do not curdle and cook. Add the lemon juice and stir well.

Pour the egg-lemon mixture back into the pot, stir and reheat slowly. Taste and adjust the salt and pepper and serve immediately.

A note on tempering: Anytime you put eggs in hot stock, always take some of the stock and mix it slowly with the eggs before pouring it into the rest of the stock. If you don't, you will have scrambled eggs.

Pasta

Cold Chinese Sesame Noodles

Anyone can have Italian pasta. Sagittarius likes to get out and see what other countries have to offer.

½ cup chicken stock
¼ cup soy sauce
4 tablespoons rice wine vinegar
1 tablespoon sesame oil
1 tablespoon sugar
½ cup cilantro, diced
2 teaspoons freshly ground black pepper
4 scallions, sliced thinly
½ red Thai chili pepper

1 cup sesame seeds
1 pound Chinese cellophane noodles
1 cup bean sprouts
¼ cup tahini sauce
1 Fuji apple, sliced thinly
1 cucumber, sliced thinly
¼ cup scallions, sliced thinly
2 teaspoons fresh ginger, diced
¼ cup peanuts, minced

Serves 8

In a large saucepan over medium heat, bring the chicken stock, soy sauce, vinegar, oil and sugar to a low boil. Stir until the sugar dissolves. Mix in the cilantro, pepper, scallions and chili pepper. Turn off the heat and let the mixture steep for about an hour. Once it cools, you can refrigerate if you aren't cooking the noodles yet. In fact, this can stay in the refrigerator, covered, for about 2 days. This needs to be cold before you serve.

Preheat the oven to 325 degrees.

Spread the sesame seeds in a single layer on a slightly greased cookie sheet. Roast in the oven about 15–20 minutes until they just start to get brown. Remove and cool.

When you are ready to serve, bring 5 cups of water to a boil. Put the noodles in a large, heatproof bowl, pour the water over them slowly, and let them stand for about 15 minutes. You can also ladle the water over the noodles if you are a precise Virgo. This is called "blooming." You will have to use a fork and gently separate them so they don't get all clumpy.

Pour the stock into the soup serving bowl and then add the sprouts, noodles, tahini, apple, cucumber, scallions, and ginger. This shouldn't be soupy at all – put just enough stock in so that it is soaked up by the noodles. Stir in the sesame seeds and then sprinkle the peanuts over top.

Veggies & Fruit
Moroccan Vegetable Tagine

A tagine is a clay pot used for cooking in many parts of Africa and the Middle East. You don't need to buy a fancy pot to make this – a Dutch oven works just as well.

1 cup couscous
½ teaspoon dried crushed red pepper
¼ teaspoon turmeric
1 ½ teaspoons kosher salt
1 teaspoon cardamom
1 teaspoon cumin
3 tablespoons extra-virgin olive oil
1 ½ cups onions, cubed
3 garlic cloves, minced
1 ¼ cups carrots, cubed
1 celery stalk, chopped

1 ½ tablespoons tomato paste
2 cups white wine
1 ¼ pounds red-skinned or
   purple potatoes, peeled, and cubed
1 pound turnips, peeled, cubed
¼ cup sun-dried tomatoes, sliced thinly
1 ½ teaspoons kosher salt
12 ounces chick peas
½ teaspoon extra-virgin olive oil
¼ cup fresh flat-leaf Italian parsley,
   chopped

A note on herbs: The best way to cut herbs is with a really sharp knife, or, if you tend to be a bit klutzy – like yours truly – have a good, sharp pair of scissors that you use for nothing else.

Serves 6

In a medium pan over medium heat combine the couscous and 4 cups of water and bring to a boil. Remove from the heat. Add the red pepper, turmeric and salt and stir well. Be gentle with it, Aries, don't smash it or mix it. Just let it be.

In a small sauté pan, heat the cardamom and cumin over low heat for 2 minutes until they just begin to brown. Remove from heat. Add the red pepper and turmeric and stir well.

In a large soup pot over medium heat, heat the oil, add the onions and cook about 5–7 minutes until they begin to lightly brown. Add the garlic and cook another minute. Add the carrots and celery and cook another 2 minutes. Stir in the tomato paste, wine, potatoes, turnips, tomatoes and toasted spices. Cook over low heat until all of the vegetables are soft – about 35–40 minutes.

While the vegetables are cooking, place the chick peas in a medium sauté pan with olive oil, cook over low heat for about 5 minutes until the peas get a little crispy. Stir the chick peas and parsley into the vegetable pot. Serve over the couscous.

Asparagus and Farro Salad

Sagittarius controls the liver and gall bladder. One food that is very good for these organs happens to also be delicious, asparagus. This recipe also uses the grain farro which appeals to the Sagittarius' love of the exotic. If you really can't find farro, use quinoa but try to find the farro. The unique taste is worth the hunt.

The farro does need to be soaked overnight so plan accordingly.

2 cups farro
3 tablespoons extra- virgin olive oil
1 pound fresh asparagus, trimmed and cut in half
2 teaspoons kosher salt
2 teaspoons freshly ground black pepper
1 cup red and yellow cherry tomatoes, halved

¾ cup raisins, chopped
¾ cup dried cranberries
½ cup fresh flat-leaf Italian parsley, chopped
1 cup chopped fresh chives
⅛ cup balsamic vinegar
1 cup Parmigiano-Reggiano cheese, shaved

Serves 8

Soak the farro in a large bowl of water overnight and then drain. Quinoa does not have to be soaked.

Preheat the oven to 450 degrees.

In a large saucepan over medium heat combine the farro and about 4 cups of water. When it boils, reduce the heat to low, cover and continue to cook for 20–30 minutes, until it is tender. Drain the farro and set aside in a large bowl.

In a medium roasting pan, pour in the oil and layer the asparagus on top. Sprinkle with the salt and pepper and turn the asparagus to be sure it has a thin coating of oil all the way around. Roast it in the oven for about 10 minutes. Check it half way through and turn the asparagus so it browns evenly.

Add the asparagus, tomatoes, raisins, cranberries, parsley and chives to the farro in a large salad bowl. Sprinkle the balsamic vinegar over top – you might need a little more than ⅛ cup but you don't want it to swim or the taste to overpower. Sprinkle the cheese over the top and serve immediately.

Meat & Fish

Linda Leduc's *Tourtiere* (Pork Pie)

My friend Linda LeDuc made this French Canadian dish a few years ago and I fell in love with it. The combination of flavors makes for a rich and satisfying winter meal – and the foreign aspect will appeal to Sagittarius.

Don't beat yourself up if you hate to make pie crust. Even Cancer cooks sometimes don't make a good crust. Take a breath. It is OK. There are many wonderful pie crusts on the market – no one will mock you if you don't make it from scratch. And if they do they don't deserve your company anyway! Tap your inner Scorpio and say to heck with them all. You have too many good friends to worry about meanies.

Make (or buy) the pie crust. See the crust recipe that follows if you want to make it yourself.

2 tablespoons butter
1 medium onion, diced
1 pound ground beef
1 pound ground pork
1 cup chicken stock (see page 44)
2 teaspoons kosher salt
1 teaspoon freshly ground black pepper
1 ½ teaspoons Old Bay seasoning

¼ teaspoon fresh sage leaves, minced
½ teaspoon fresh thyme, minced
½ teaspoon ground cloves
1 pinch cinnamon
8 Ritz crackers, rolled into fine crumbs
   or ¼ cup cornmeal
1 egg, beaten

Serves 6 – 8

Preheat the oven to 425 degrees.

Line the bottom of a 1 quart casserole with pie crust.

In a medium sauté pan, heat the butter and add the onion. Cook about 5 minutes until the onion is clear. Add the meat, frying only until brown. Add the stock, just enough to allow the meat to peek through. Let this simmer for about 10 minutes. Add seasonings and herbs. Start adding the crumbs or cornmeal, using a fork. Add only enough crumbs to make a light, fluffy mixture.

Pour the mixture into the casserole and smooth it over the crust. Cover with upper crust and brush the crust with the egg. Bake for 30–35 minutes.

Pie crust

2 sticks unsalted butter, ice cold
    and cut into 1 inch slices, divided
3 cups all-purpose flour

2 teaspoons kosher salt
1 teaspoon sugar
½–¾ cup ice water

Makes a top and bottom crust.

Put the butter in the freezer for about 10 minutes after you cut it.

Combine the flour, salt and sugar and 1 stick of the butter in a food processor and pulse until they come together and just start to make little balls. This takes about 8–10 minutes. Then pulse in the other stick of butter until the little balls are formed and about the size of a raspberry.

Pulse in the ice water until it is fully mixed in. The dough should be holding together easily. Dump it out on a lightly floured board and roll into a ball. Wrap in plastic wrap and refrigerate for 30 minutes.

Cut the dough in half. Roll each piece on a well-floured board into a circle, rolling from the center to the edge. Turn the dough and then roll again. Keep turning and rolling until the dough is about 11 inches. Grab your casserole and put it near the dough. Fold the dough in half, place in the casserole, and unfold to fit the pan. Repeat with the top crust.

Bibimbap

Pronounced –"BEE-beem-bop"

Anything foreign will appeal to the Sag. And this is a great meal that my friend Marge Cox Epstein has served many times. Her husband, Ken, spent years in the Peace Corps in Korea and they have both become wonderful cooks of the cuisine. *Bibimbap* is a favorite of the region. Don't be afraid of the strange names – it is easy and delicious.

The *bulgogi* should marinate at least 4 hours; overnight is best so plan accordingly.

For the *bulgogi* (Korean marinated and grilled beef)

2 pounds rib eye steak, sliced thinly*
3 tablespoons sugar, divided
2 tablespoons rice vinegar
3 tablespoons soy sauce
1 tablespoon rice wine
1 garlic clove, minced

¼ teaspoon fresh ginger, minced
1 scallion, diced
2 teaspoons sesame oil
½ teaspoon freshly ground black pepper
1 small white onion, diced

Serves 8

♈ ♉ ♊ ♋ ♌ ♍ ♎ ♏ ♐ ♑ ♒ ♓

For *Bibimbap*

2 cups steamed white rice – try to get
  traditional Korean white rice
Bulgogi (see page 208)
2 carrots, julienned
  (for more bite mix in 1 daikon radish, julienned)
2 cups cooked bean sprouts, sautéed in a
  little sesame oil and seasoned with salt
2 cups cooked spinach, sautéed in a little
  sesame or peanut oil and seasoned with salt

2 cups thin green beans, sautéed in a little sesame oil.
1 egg, cooked over easy
1 tablespoon sesame seeds
1 tablespoon dark sesame oil
Soy sauce, to taste
Gochuchang paste (available at Korean market)

In a medium bowl toss the rib eye with 2 tablespoons each of sugar and rice vinegar. In a small bowl, combine the soy sauce, the remaining sugar, rice wine, garlic, fresh ginger, scallion, sesame oil, pepper, white onion and 1 tablespoon water.

Pour the soy sauce mixture over the sliced meat and let it marinate for at least 1 hour.

When you are ready to serve, grill the meat over indirect coals until brown on both sides – about 1–2 minutes per side or put in a single layer under a low broiler until brown.

Put the cooked rice in large slightly shallow bowl. Place the *bulgogi* (with juices from cooked meat) and veggies on top of the rice. Put the egg on top. Sprinkle with sesame seeds and drizzle with sesame oil, Gochuchang and soy sauce.

*You can also use thinly sliced chicken instead of beef or half chicken, half beef.

A note on julienne: Don't let words spook you. All julienned means is to cut into fine strips like matchsticks. The food won't suffer if they are a bit thicker. Cooking should be fun. Hear that, Virgo? Fun. Don't get hung up on fancy terms.

To Their Health

Salmon Cakes

Sagittarius rules the hip and thigh area. They often suffer from arthritic issues caused by over exertion and sports related injuries. They need to guard against inflammation. Salmon is a great anti-inflammatory food. These fast and tasty cakes are perfect for the Sagittarius on the run and they are usually always on the run.

1 tablespoon extra-virgin olive oil
1 celery stalk, minced
1 small white onion, minced
12 ounces canned salmon, minced
1 8-ounce can of corn
2 tablespoons flat leaf Italian parsley, minced
1 tablespoon Dijon mustard

1 teaspoon kosher salt
1 teaspoon freshly ground black pepper
1 large egg
½ cup bread crumbs, (if you use gluten free or whole-wheat crumbs you may have to add more mustard to make them moist.)

Serves 6

Preheat the oven to 400 degrees.

Heat the olive oil in a medium sauté pan over medium heat. Add the celery and onion and sauté for about 6–8 minutes until the onion is translucent.

Flake the salmon in a medium bowl removing any skin and bones. Add the celery, onion, corn, parsley, mustard, salt, pepper, egg and bread crumbs and mix together. Form the mixture into 1 by 2 inch patties.

Spray a long baking pan with olive oil spray. Gently place the cakes in the pan and cook for 15–20 minutes. Check half way through – if the tops are brown, flip them over. Cakes should be lightly browned on both sides.

Serve immediately.

A note on olive oil: I use it for just about everything even baking sometimes. I always heard, but never believed, the story that you can't fry with olive oil because it burns too quickly. I was vindicated in my belief recently when new studies in Jaen, Spain confirmed that olive oil is better than canola or any other for frying.

Opposites Attract: Stretching Your Sagittarius South Node

The opposite sign to Sagittarius is Gemini. Sag. is the deep thinker and the searcher. Gemini just wants to gather information for information's sake. Sometimes Sag. gets so bogged down in the deep thoughts of the universe they forget how to communicate – how to exchange that information – how to get off the lofty mountain. They need a little bit of Gemini verbal acuity to spread that information around! So whip up some Chinese tea eggs and get the Sag. talking about these pretty finger foods and soon enough they will come down off their cloud and tell you what they have learned.

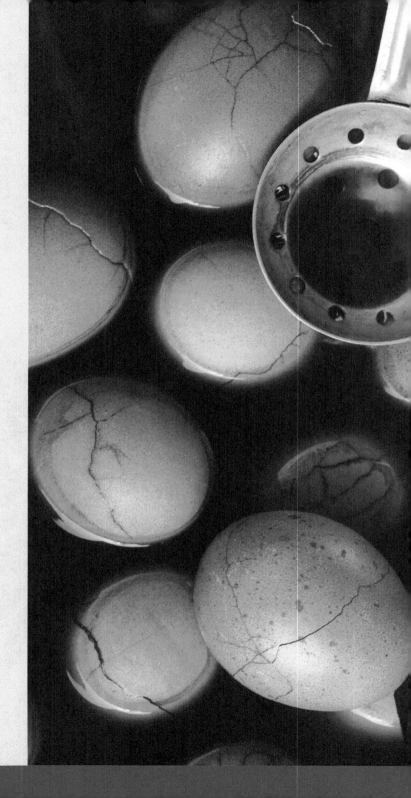

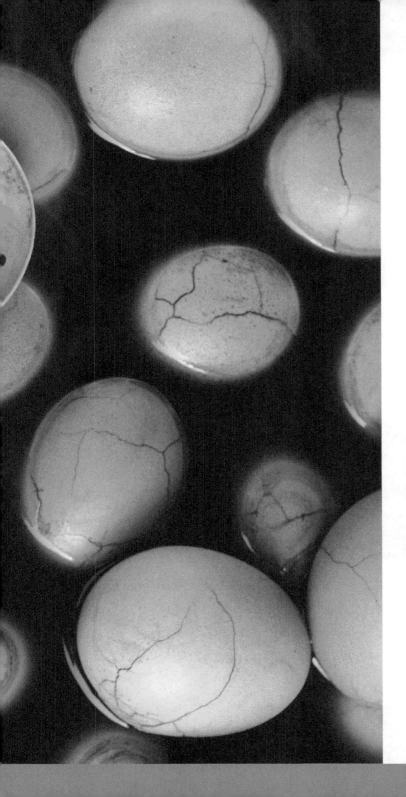

Chinese Tea Eggs

These eggs must be refrigerated overnight, so plan accordingly.

> 8 large eggs
> 3 cups brewed strong black tea, cooled
> ½ cups dark soy sauce
> 5 pieces star anise
> ½ tablespoon cinnamon
>
> Serves 8

The darker the tea and soy sauce, the prettier these eggs will be.

Place the eggs in a medium sauce pan and add enough water to just cover them. Bring to a boil, turn off the heat, cover and allow them to stand for at least 30 minutes. Pour out the water; fill the pan with cold water. When the eggs are cool to the touch pour out the water. Tap each one with the back of a teaspoon and gently crack the shells. Don't peel or let the shells fall off – just crack them.

Return the cracked eggs to the pan, pour in the tea and add the other ingredients. Bring to a boil reduce heat and simmer for an hour. Add water or more tea if it gets dry. Remove from heat, cool and place the pan in the refrigerator overnight. Be sure the eggs are submerged in the tea.

When you are ready to eat, peel and serve

A note on noodles and pastas: Ideally you should take your pasta noodles and toss them directly into whatever sauce you are making. Never –ever run pasta under cold water to cool. That removes all of the starch and the sauce runs right off. When you have to mix the noodles into a salad or other cool dish, just shake them around for a second or two to air cool and stir in quickly.

Dessert

Noodle *Kugel*

One of the things Sagittarius searches the world for is religious truth. They like to experience various cultures and religions to find what their own truth is. Why not give them a "religious" dessert? Noodle kugels are often prepared at holiday meals in Ashkenazi Jewish homes. Some Hasidic Jews believe that eating kugel on the Sabbath bestows special blessings. I use thin noodles instead of the traditional fat noodles and added mascarpone instead of sour cream.

1 stick unsalted butter, plus more to grease the dish
2 tablespoons kosher salt, divided
12 ounces egg noodles
3 large eggs
2 cups cottage cheese

Serves 6 – 8

2 cups mascarpone cheese
2 cups whole milk
⅛ teaspoon ground cinnamon
½ teaspoon orange zest, grated
½ teaspoon freshly ground black pepper

Preheat the oven to 350 degrees. Butter a 3-quart baking dish.

Bring about 4 quarters of water and 1 tablespoon of the salt to a boil over high heat in a medium saucepan. Add the noodles and cook until *al dente* – about 6 minutes. Meanwhile, pulse the eggs, cottage cheese, mascarpone, milk, cinnamon, orange zest and the rest of the salt in a food processor until smooth. Pour into a large mixing bowl. Drain the noodles. After they cool to the touch, add them to the bowl, season with the pepper and toss. Don't wait until they become a clumpy mess.

Transfer the mixture to the 3 quart baking dish and bake until just set, 35–40 minutes. Let the kugel rest 10 minutes before serving. Store any extra in the refrigerator but bring to room temperature before serving. To me it makes it taste better.

Famous People with
Sagittarius South Node – Gemini North Node

Arnold Schwarzenegger –

This is a perfect example of a person stuck in their own Sagittarius truth. HE knows what is right and wrong and will listen little to others. The over-reaching and the bombast are all indicative of someone who has stayed in the Sagittarius shadow for a bit too long. Yeah and those crazy muscles early-on in his career were very much a Jupiter expansion thing. He once tweeted that his favorite food was steak barbequed on the grill. That sounds big, juicy and very Sagittarian.

Bill Clinton –

Again someone who oversteps a bit, and can be over confident. However, we can see him use the Gemini gift of speech to embrace broad ideals that can be seen as a spiritual quest to help people around the world with his Clinton Global Initiative. We know that he loved to have junk food in excess when in the White House. However, after some serious illness that probably reminded him that his father died even before he was born, Clinton has toned down his eating habits a lot and has reigned in his Jupiterian excessiveness.

Sagittarius North Node Angelina Jolie who did a very Sagittarius
thing by adopting children from foreign countries, claims that
she and her children just love to eat crickets. While that
creeps out most Americans, it is a delicacy in many
parts of the world like these Thai fried crickets.

capricorn

Chapter 12

The slow and steady Goat epitomizes Capricorn (although she is traditionally a sea goat – so your goat may have an affinity for the water as well as the mountain). Capricorns like tradition, rules and organization and they thrive on history, politics and international debate.

Capricorn vibrates to the 10th house, the house traditionally assigned to the father and the one that controls authority figures such as governmental authority. Saturn, its ruler, was often described as a malefic planet. That is a bit too "cut-and-dried" for me. Without Saturn we would have anarchy with no structure at all, even in our bodies. Saturn keeps things in check.

Positive aspects of Capricorn include:
organizational ability, the ability to meet goals, and being good providers for those in their care.

Shadow aspects of Capricorn include:
depression, over- attention to duty at the expense of fun and whimsy, and over-scheduling.

Foodie aspects of Capricorn include:
foods that are substantial, hearty and practical. You have to introduce fun to the goat diet
– but not hit them over the head with it. They can't be seen as being frivolous after all!

Famous People with Capricorn Rising

Abraham Lincoln – With his Moon also in Capricorn, President Lincoln was subjected to long bouts of "melancholia." He was by no means a foodie and absent-mindedly munched on apples. His wife would go to great lengths to have the few foods he did like on hand just so he would eat something.

Michelangelo – Food was not often on the mind of this dedicated Capricorn. He would paint and sculpt for days oblivious to his bodily needs. He is the perfect example of the structure that Capricorn can bring even from big hunks of shapeless marble.

Appetizer

Shrimp and Scallop Ceviche

Although we think of goats as mountain creatures and an Earth Sign, the mythological Capricorn is a water creature. I personally feel that the plodding goat would like nothing more than to jump into the sea and freely swim about. Yet they tie themselves to work and duty. So let's start off with a little morsel from the sea to remind them of the fun they can have in the water.

Of course, Capricorn will balk at just the idea of scallops and shrimp – a good piece of carp is all they need! Start off by telling them about the plight of the fishing industry, that fish is "made in America." This will appeal to their patriotic, paternal side. As they start to wax on about economics or some such topic shove a fork of this into their mouths. While they will never admit it, they will like this bit of whimsy.

8 tablespoons lemon juice
4 tablespoons lime juice
3 tablespoons orange juice
1 teaspoon soy sauce
¾ pound scallops
1 pound medium shrimp, cleaned and deveined

Serves 6

1 teaspoon ginger, minced
2 teaspoons garlic, minced
⅛ cup flat leaf Italian parsley, finely chopped
¼ cup red onions, finely chopped
½ medium red pepper, diced
½ medium green pepper, diced

In a medium bowl, whisk together the citrus juices and soy sauce. Stir in the fish, ginger and garlic, making sure that the fish is fully coated. Cover and refrigerate for at least 3 hours.

One half hour before serving, stir in the parsley, onions and peppers.

A note on cleaning scallops: If you buy fresh scallops carefully pry them open. It is best to hold the top with a thick towel in case your knife slips. Make sure that you detach the muscle from the scallop and toss the top shell with the muscle attachment away. You should get rid of any black portions. Wash the scallop after you remove the bottom shell. You don't want any sand or grit in your dish.

Soup

Cabbage Soup

This is another one from my friend Marge Cox Epstein. She said she messed around with it until it tasted right and you should, too. (She is an Aquarius, not a Capricorn by any means.) If it seems too thin, add a little soy sauce. You can add or garnish with sour cream. Capricorn will appreciate the good, hearty taste of this soup and how quick it is to prepare. After all, we can't waste time on food – it is something just to keep body and soul together, you know! When Capricorn starts up like this just nod every five minutes to make them feel like you are listening and go about chopping your cabbage.

2 tablespoons extra-virgin olive oil
8-10 cups cabbage, roughly chopped
2 large onions, diced
3 tablespoons flour
3-4 cups chicken stock (see recipe on page 44)
2 28-ounce cans diced tomatoes
2 teaspoons kosher salt
½ teaspoon freshly ground black pepper
2-3 tablespoons fresh lemon juice
2 teaspoons caraway seeds
1 cup sour cream (optional)

Serve 8 – 10

A note on cabbage: Cabbages tend to be big and sometimes you just have a lot left around after your dish is done. Just quickly par boil it, drain, put in a plastic bag and freeze until you need more. It is remarkably hardy. I have also done this with cauliflower and broccoli.

In a large sauté pan heat the oil over medium heat. Add the cabbage and onions and sauté until the onions are translucent and cabbage starts to soften, approximately 20 minutes. Add a little more oil if the pan begins to run dry. Watch your heat. If the food is drying out quickly your heat is up too high.

Sprinkle in the flour and gradually add the chicken stock, stirring constantly until the soup starts to boil. Reduce the heat and add the tomatoes, salt, pepper, lemon juice and caraway seeds. Cover and cook over low heat for at least an hour, stirring often.

Just before serving, dollop the sour cream on top.

Pasta

Dan Dan Noodles

Capricorns are very interested in international affairs. Normal pasta dishes will quickly lose their appeal. These Chinese *Dan Dan* noodles pack a kick and will remind Capricorns of their days in international espionage – even if their service was limited to reading a Ludlum thriller.

A note on scallions, shallots, onions, etc.: If you have two bags of shallots left over and a recipe calls for scallions, use the shallots. Taste your food. You may have to put a few more or a few less in but I am a big believer in using what you have. The one caution would be to watch red onions. They pack a punch. The same thing is true with peppers. Don't add habaneros when a recipe calls for sweet banana peppers.

2 tablespoons extra-virgin olive oil
¼ cup scallions, minced
10 ounces ground pork
12 ounces udon noodles
3 garlic cloves, minced
1 teaspoon fresh ginger, minced
1 teaspoon chili paste
¼ cup chicken or vegetable stock
  (see recipe on page 44)
2 ounces soy sauce
¼ cup white wine

Serves 6

Heat 2 tablespoons of oil in a medium saucepan over medium heat; add the scallions and sauté about 2 minutes. Add the pork and continue to cook stirring often until the pork is lightly browned.

While the pork is browning, cook the udon noodles in large pot of boiling water, for about 6 minutes or until *al dente*. Drain and pour into a large bowl.

Add the garlic and ginger to the pork and continue to cook another 2 minutes. Stir in the chili paste, chicken stock, soy sauce and white wine. Cook down until the liquid is reduced by half.

Toss the pork mixture over the noodles, stir well and serve immediately.

Veggies & Fruit

Old Fashioned "Pympkin Pie"

I read that food historians think the original pumpkin pie was a pumpkin stuffed with apples, butter and milk. Sugar was added if you could afford it. Pumpkins are good for Capricorn; they are sturdy and remind us of Pilgrims! I used the original old-time spelling of pumpkin here because it will probably make the Capricorn rush to their library to re-read their books on Old English writing!

1 medium sugar pumpkin
3 medium apples, cored and diced
1 cup raisins
2 tablespoons butter

Serves 4 – 6

¼ cup sugar
1 teaspoon cinnamon
1 teaspoon freshly grated nutmeg
½ cup apple cider

Preheat the oven to 350 degrees.

Place the pumpkin on a lightly greased roasting pan and cook for about 30 minutes, until it is barely soft. When it is cooled to the touch, remove the stem, and remove the seeds and string. (See page 90 for my tip on pumpkin seeds.)

In a medium saucepan over medium heat combine the apples, raisins, butter, sugar, cinnamon, nutmeg and apple cider. Cook for about 15 minutes until most of the cider is gone, stirring often to prevent sticking.

Spoon the apple mixture into the pumpkin and return it to the oven. Cook for another 20 minutes. To serve, slice the pumpkin as you would a pie. Serve warm.

Black Beans a

Capricorns can get themselves so woun
Capricorn moods can turn dark becaus
orderly fashion. Needless to say, they g
Capricorn) is to learn what areas of life t
be prone to depression, in the 2nd, they

Black beans have lots of vitamin B whi

Note that if you use dried beans you w

>1 pound dried black beans
>⅛ cup extra-virgin olive oil
>2 green bell peppers, diced and
>1 red pepper, diced and seeded
>1 medium white onion, diced
>3 garlic cloves, diced
>
>Serves 6 – 8

Soak the beans in 4 quarts of water ove
which don't need to be soaked. I think
cheaper but my Gemini doesn't always

Heat the oil in a medium saucepan ove
onion, garlic, oregano and cumin and s
start to brown and the onions begin to
of water and bring to a boil, stirring oft
the heat to simmer and cook the mixtu

Add the wine, salt and pepper to the b
immediately reduce the heat to a simm

Continue to simmer, uncovered, until t
hours.

Serve over the rice.

A note on pearl onions:
worries. Simply cut off
enough water to cover t
cool enough to handle,
into a bowl. Those suck
– but where is the sport

Some people hate using them because they are hard to peel. No
he root end and then place the onions in a saucepan with just
em. Bring to a boil for about two minutes. Drain them and when
queeze the onions gently to slip off the skins. Make sure you do this
rs can really fly. You can also buy them frozen and already prepped
in that?

Meat & Fish

Yankee Pot Roast

Capricorns don't like frills. They like "real" food. There are many recipes for Yankee Pot Roast but I always liked my Moms addition of tomato sauce because it made it tastier and the meat more tender. This addition will appeal to the Capricorn's love of tradition.

¼ cup extra-virgin olive oil
4 teaspoons kosher salt
4 teaspoons freshly ground black pepper
4–5 pounds chuck or bottom round roast
2 large carrots, chopped
2 celery stalks, chopped
2 onions, chopped
4–5 garlic cloves, minced

6 sprigs fresh thyme, minced
4 cups chicken stock (see recipe on page 44)
2 cups red wine
2 tablespoons tomato paste
1 cup tomato sauce
1 bag pearl onions
1 pound new potatoes, halved
1 pound button mushrooms, quartered

Serves 8

Preheat the oven to 325 degrees.

Heat a large Dutch oven over medium heat; add the olive oil. Salt and pepper both sides of the roast. Brown the meat about 2 minutes on each side. Remove the meat to a platter. Pour off all but 2 tablespoons of oil. Reduce the heat to medium and add the carrots, celery, onions and the garlic and cook about 5 minutes until the garlic begins to brown. Add the thyme, chicken stock, wine, tomato paste, sauce and the meat.

Cover and place the Dutch oven in the oven and cook for 2–3 hours. Check every hour to be sure the meat is well covered with liquid. Add more wine or stock as necessary.

Two hours before serving, stir in the pearl onions, potatoes and mushrooms. Cover and return to oven.

To serve, slice the beef, and arrange the vegetables around it, pour the liquid over the top until well moistened. Serve extra liquid on the side.

Paella

There are a ton of paella recipes because they vary from region to region of Spain. You can use almost any combination of sausage, chicken and fish or make it all fish or all meat! The heartiness of the meal will appeal to Capricorn's need for solid food. You may have to endure an hour or two of his take on Spanish history but the taste will make it worth the hassle.

1–4 pound chicken, cut into serving pieces, patted dry
2 teaspoons kosher salt
2 teaspoons freshly ground black pepper
6 tablespoons extra-virgin olive oil
5 chorizo sausages, sliced ¼-inch thick
1 cup white onions, minced
2 medium red bell peppers seeded, and cut into strips
1 28-ounce can crushed tomatoes
3 garlic cloves, minced
1 tablespoon fresh thyme, minced
1 tablespoon fresh flat-leaf Italian parsley, minced

1 tablespoon paprika
3 cups long-grain rice
¼ teaspoon saffron threads
5 to 6 cups chicken stock (see page 44)
12 extra-large shrimp, shelled and deveined
12 hard-shelled clams, such as littlenecks, scrubbed
12 mussels, scrubbed and debearded
½ pound of calamari, cleaned
1 cup white wine
1 cup peas

Serves 4

Preheat the oven to 400 degrees.

Season the chicken with salt and pepper. Heat the oil in a large oven proof sauté or paella pan over medium heat. Add the chicken and cook about 2–3 minutes on each side until it is nicely browned. Add the sausages and cook about 2 minutes on each side. Transfer the chicken and sausage to a platter. Add the onions, and peppers to the pan and sauté for 5 minutes. Add tomatoes, garlic, thyme, parsley and paprika and cook, stirring, for 5 minutes more.

Add the rice, saffron and stock to the pan and bring to a boil over high heat. Remove the pan from the heat and let the rice rest for about 20 minutes. Then arrange the chicken and sausage on top of the rice. Cook in the oven for 45 minutes or until the rice is soft. Add the shrimp, clams, mussels, calamari, wine and peas and more stock if needed; return to the oven and cook another 15–20 minutes until the clams and mussels are open. You don't have to make this a masterpiece although signs ruled by Venus might want to spend hours arranging and rearranging the meat and fish. People do get hungry so please try to refrain!

Serve immediately. Don't forget to scrape the bottom of the dish and get all of the good crust on the bottom called *socarrat*.

To Their Health

Capricorns need to step away from the work, history, plans and just climbing that mountain in general in order to nurture their more emotional side. The opposite sign to Capricorn is Cancer – the sign of emotions, Mom, home-hearth and all things warm and fuzzy. Speaking of fuzzy, – let's give our Capricorn some peaches and champagne to help them remember there is more than duty in this world.

Peaches and Champagne

4 large ripe, white peaches
4 cups champagne
½ cup water
1 clove
½ cup sugar

Serves 4

½ small vanilla bean
1 pint strawberries
1 cup whipping cream
4 large mint or basil leaves

Fill a medium sized dish with ice water.

Heat a large pot of water over medium heat. Make small crisscross cuts on top of each peach. With a slotted spoon drop them into the water. Keep them in the water about 1 minute just long enough to loosen the skin, and then gently lift from the pot into the dish of ice water. Remove all of the peach skins. Cut the peaches in half and remove the pit.

Combine the champagne, water, clove, sugar and vanilla bean in a medium pot. Turn the heat to high, bring to a boil and then reduce to simmer. Add the peaches to the water and simmer for 8–10 minutes. Remove from heat and allow to cool.

In a food processor puree the strawberries. Beat the cream with an electric mixer until it becomes whipped cream – depending on your machine that can take 5–10 minutes. Pour the cream into the food processor and blend the berries and cream together.

To serve place the peachs on a dessert dish. Place a dollop of the strawberry cream on top and decorate with the mint leaves. Serve immediately with glasses of champagne!

Opposites Attract:
Stretching Your
Capricorn South Node

Capricorn South Node people have to learn how to play. They are always so caught up with duty and structure and order that they just need to let their hair down and goof around for a while. That is why I am suggesting that you just have a fun picnic in the house for your Capricorn. I don't care if you live on top of a snowy mountain, throw a rug on the floor, import a little sand if you can, put on your Bermuda shorts and floppy straw hat and surprise your goat with an indoor picnic. You can even cut out some black ants and a big old yellow Sun. Don't forget to put on some beach music and break out the paper (or reusable plastic plates.)

If you have a fireplace, start a "beach bonfire" and bury some unhusked corn on the floor of the fireplace away from direct flame. It should be cooked – depending on how hot the fire is – in 15–30 minutes. Get some long forks and roast hot dogs over the flames. If you don't have a fireplace, make the hotdogs, corn and some potato salad ahead of time. Add a nice strawberry salad or even a green salad and some cookies. Place them in a big picnic basket and have them ready to go when your Capricorn comes through the door.

After you get your Capricorn to loosen their tie and do something as "foolish" as have an indoor picnic, lay out the food and then give them the fun ending surprise. Make some popcorn! You can make the cheese mixture in advance and toss it after you have popped the corn. (Again, you can pop it on an open fire but you must have a special popcorn popper designed to work over an open fire to do it safely.) You can make this up to two hours before you serve it. If you are really lucky your Capricorn might get so relaxed you might actually have a food fight.

Picnic in the House with Adult Popcorn

¼ cup Parmigiano-Reggiano cheese, grated
2 teaspoons kosher salt
¾ teaspoon cayenne pepper
½ teaspoon cumin
¼ cup butter, melted
1 cup popcorn, unpopped

Serves 4

In a food processor pulse together the cheese, salt, cayenne, and cumin. Once it is mixed, run the processor for about 2 minutes until it is very fine. Pop the corn and immediately toss with the butter. Once the corn is coated with butter, toss it with the cheese mix.

A note on popcorn: Oh do be careful when purchasing popcorn. So much of it is made with bad oils and hydrogenated garbage. Read the bag, It should have very few ingredients, the key one being corn!

Dessert

Rum Raisin Rice Pudding

This rice pudding is not only comforting but has that sense of history the Capricorn will so love. This is adapted from a recipe I found long ago that purported to be Thomas Jefferson's Rice Pudding. You can dress it up by serving with some whole cinnamon sticks on the side.

Butter-flavored cooking spray works best for this recipe so be sure to have it on hand if you normally use the olive oil type.

4 large eggs
¾ cup sugar
2 ½ cups milk
2 cups cooked brown or white rice
2 teaspoons lemon juice

Serves 8

1 ½ teaspoons pure vanilla extract
½ cup butter, melted
1 teaspoon freshly grated nutmeg
1 cup seedless raisins
½ cup light rum

Preheat the oven to 350 degrees.

Spray the bottom of a 3-quart baking dish with a generous amount of butter-flavored cooking spray.

In a large bowl, beat the eggs with the sugar and milk. Gently stir in the rice, lemon juice, vanilla, melted butter, nutmeg, raisins and rum.

Pour the mixture into the baking dish. Then place the casserole in a large roasting pan. Fill the pan with boiling water half way up the side of the baking dish.

Bake until the pudding is set in the center – about 45 minutes. Let it cool on a cooling rack before serving. I like rice pudding at room temperature. You can store it in the refrigerator for a few days, but bring up to room temperature before serving.

Famous People with
Capricorn South Node –
Cancer North Node

Michelle Obama –

I feel she is making great strides towards reaching her North Node. She is close to – and wields a great deal of government power (Capricorn), yet she has crafted the role of being the Nation's mother (Cancer) by telling children how to eat to be well.

Adolph Hitler –

Yes, from the sublime to the horrible. However, this is a perfect illustration of one person sailing gracefully toward her North Node, and a monster deeply stuck in the shadow of his South; dictatorial, authoritarian power. It is purported that Hitler was a vegetarian, something that is disputed by some current research. However, there are many reports that his table manners were horrible, indicating further his total lack of concern for anyone stuck within his energy field.

It might have just been political hype but I understand Capricorn North Node President John Kennedy's favorites included traditional, hearty New England clam chowder.

aquarius
Chapter 13

Aquarians are all about freedom. They have to feel unfettered. Emotionally attaching to something or someone is hard for them because they always feel that it limits their freedom. They can appear friendly but remote. President Obama is Aquarius rising and it always cracks me up when people say he is distant or can't connect. Of course, he appears that way – he is projecting with Aquarian energy.

The friendliness comes from their vibration to the 11th house, the house of social contacts and group humanitarian efforts. They really do care about the betterment of all mankind; it is just relating one-on-one that makes them nervous.

Aquarius is always pushing us into the future. They see twenty years, heck they live twenty years ahead of the rest of society. They are the astrological canary in the coal mine.

There is something very unique about Aquarians. It could be that their ruling planet Uranus is the only one to rotate on its side rather than more or less right-side-up.

Positive aspects of Aquarius include:
friendliness, true humanitarianism and a deep sense that we are all brothers and sisters.

Shadow aspects of Aquarius include:
sudden and unpredicted changes to their emotions, detachment, and coldness.

Foodie aspects of Aquarius include:
the love of sustainable foods, unique foods and foods they
share with their vast and interesting array of friends.

Famous People with Aquarius Rising

Henry David Thoreau – In a hunt-and-eat, meat-and-potatoes era Thoreau, like many Aquarians, was ahead of his time. In *Walden* he wrote, "It may be vain to ask why the imagination will not be reconciled to flesh and fat. I am satisfied that it is not. Is it not a reproach that man is a carnivorous animal? True, he can and does live, in a great measure, by preying on other animals; but this is a miserable way – as anyone who will go to snaring rabbits, or slaughtering lambs, may learn – and he will be regarded as a benefactor of his race who shall teach man to confine himself to a more innocent and wholesome diet."

Whoopi Goldberg – If you change your name to "Whoopi Goldberg" you have to have Aquarius prominently in your chart. When asked by CNN's Piers Morgan what was her favorite food she gave a wonderfully Aquarian off-the-wall answer. "I don't like food that can be hiding something." I love it. She also hates creamed corn, not finding the "point" of it.

Appetizer

Fried Goat Cheese Balls

I read recently that food trends of the next few years will feature small tasteful morsels that can be quickly popped into the mouth. What would be better than to give our future-minded Aquarian friends something that is ahead of the food curve?

These can stay in the refrigerator overnight before cooking, so plan accordingly.

1 10-ounce log fresh goat cheese
1 large egg, lightly beaten
½ cup club soda
¾ cup all-purpose flour
1 teaspoon kosher salt

Serves 6

3 cups panko, lightly crushed (you can use
    regular bread crumbs if you can't find panko)
½ teaspoon red pepper flakes
¼ cup honey or agave nectar
¼ cup extra-virgin olive oil
    (or canola if you prefer to fry with that)

Cut the goat cheese log into 16 pieces and roll each into a ball. Place them on a cookie sheet that has been lined with wax paper or parchment and refrigerate for 4 hours or overnight.

In a medium bowl, whisk together the egg and club soda and then slowly whisk in the flour and salt. Set aside.

Pour the panko or bread crumbs into a large bowl. Dip the balls first into the flour mixture and then roll around in the panko until they have a fine coat all the way around.

If you aren't going to serve them right away you can return the balls to the refrigerator for up to 1 hour.

Just before serving, mix the red pepper and honey together in a serving bowl.

Heat the olive oil in a medium sauté pan over medium heat. To test the oil, sprinkle in a little of the panko; if it lightly bubbles, the oil is ready. Fry the balls in the oil, until lightly brown on each side – about 1 minute on each side. Remove to a platter that is covered with paper towels. A slotted spoon works best. Transfer to a serving platter and serve immediately with the red pepper sauce on the side.

Soup

Pho

I love *pho*, especially the wonderful stock. I love it with beef, but if your Aquarius is a vegetarian (as they just might be) you can make it with a veggie stock. Simply sauté some celery, carrots and kale (about two cups each) in some extra-virgin olive oil until the carrots and celery are lightly browned – about 5 minutes. And leave the beef out, of course.

This soup needs to sit overnight, so plan accordingly. Do try to make this beef stock instead of using the packaged stuff. For *pho* it really makes a difference.

5 pieces star anise
3 whole cloves
2 tablespoons extra-virgin olive oil
2 medium yellow onions, diced
4-inch piece ginger, minced
5-6 pounds beef soup bones
   (any good butcher should have these)
½ pound beef chuck, rump, brisket
   or cross rib roast
1 ½ tablespoons kosher salt
4 tablespoons fish sauce
1 tablespoon sugar
2 pounds rice stick noodles (if you don't have any Asian
   stores around you, substitute any thin noodle)

Serves 6 – 8

¾ pound raw eye of round, sirloin, London broil
   or tri-tip steak, sliced thinly across the grain
   ($^1/_{16}$ inch thick)
4 scallions, green part only, cut into thin rings
⅓ cup cilantro, chopped
½ teaspoon freshly ground black pepper

Optional Garnishes

Spearmint (*hung lui*) and Asian/Thai
basil (*hung que*) sprigs
Leaves of thorny cilantro (*ngo gai*)
½ pound bean sprouts
2 red hot chilies, minced
4 limes, wedged

In a small sauté pan over low heat place the anise and cloves. Allow them to just heat for about 30 seconds, shake the pan and heat another 30 seconds. Remove from the heat and set aside.

Heat the oil in a large stock pot over medium heat and add the onions and ginger. Sauté until the onions are translucent – about 8–10 minutes. Pour in 6 quarts of water and add the bones, chuck and salt. Bring to a boil and then reduce the heat to simmer. Add the fish sauce and sugar. Skim the surface often to remove any foam and fat and simmer uncovered for about an hour and a half.

Wrap the star anise and cloves in a piece of cheesecloth and add to the stock. Allow the stock to simmer another hour uncovered. Turn off the heat and allow the stock to cool to room temperature. Strain through a fine sieve and remove and toss any gelatinous and other yucky material and any chunks of onion, ginger or spices that might remain.

Place the stock in a large bowl, cover and refrigerate overnight. The next morning skim off any remaining fat that has collected on the top.

When you are ready to serve, prepare any of the optional garnishes and place them on serving trays and bowls. Bring the stock to a low boil over medium heat. Bring 4 quarts of water to a boil over high heat in a medium stock pot, add the noodles and blanch for about 30 seconds. (If you are using non-Asian noodles, – cook them for about 5 minutes.) Drain the noodles and divide them into serving bowls if you are doing individual bowls or into the soup tureen.

Add the thinly sliced meat, scallions, cilantro and pepper. Pour the stock into the serving bowl(s) and serve immediately.

A note on cutting meat thinly: Freeze the meat for at least 15 minutes before cutting.

It makes the knife go through much easier and you get thinner slices.

Pasta

Fried Pasta

Anyone can boil pasta, but you want to change things up for your revolutionary Aquarian!

    3 tablespoons kosher salt
    1 ½ pounds thin spaghetti – but not angel hair
    ¼ cup extra-virgin olive oil
    3 garlic cloves, minced
    1 teaspoon red pepper flakes
    5 tablespoons basil pesto (see page 33)
    ¾ cup ricotta cheese
    10 sprigs fresh basil

    Serves 8

In a large soup pan, add 3 quarts of water and the salt and bring to a boil over high heat. Add the spaghetti and reduce heat to medium. Cook, stirring often about 8–10 minutes until *al dente*.

While the pasta is cooking, heat the olive oil in a large sauté pan over medium heat. Add the garlic and cook until it just begins to brown. Stir in the red pepper flakes. When the spaghetti is cooked, drain well and pour into the frying pan. Stir in the pesto, being sure to coat the spaghetti well. Lower the heat and cook the spaghetti for 4 minutes, flip it over and cook on the other side another 4 minutes.

Turn the spaghetti into a platter, dollop the ricotta cheese on top and decorate with basil.

Veggies & Fruit

Watermelon Basket

I remember making these for several dates in the late '70's and early '80's when I was in my "impress the guys stage." Sadly, these melon baskets have fallen out of fashion but I would like to see them come back. They are pretty and fun and are just what your Aquarian needs to entertain their hordes of friends.

There are thousands of ways to cut the watermelon and many ways to be fancy; I am not particularly artistic so I do the basics only. Taurus, Librans and possibly Cancers will be making beautiful artistic baskets. Virgos and Capricorns will be making sturdy, sane structures and Leos will have their staffs doing it!

1 large oblong watermelon
2 large cantaloupes
1 fresh pineapple
1 quart fresh strawberries
1 pint fresh blueberries

1 pint fresh raspberries
2 cups green grapes
2 cups fresh orange juice
½ cup fresh mint leaves, diced

Serves 10 – 15

Cut a thin slice from the bottom of watermelon with a sharp knife so that it sits flat. Mark a horizontal cutting line all around the watermelon at the center with a pencil. Make the handle of the basket by making vertical cuts down the center of the melon to the horizontal pencil line. Be sure to leave a 1 ½ inch handle in the center. With a long sharp knife, cut all the way through the rind above the horizontal line in a zigzag pattern. Don't cut the handles off. Carefully lift off the side pieces.

Remove the insides of the watermelon, cantaloupes and pineapple with a melon baller and place in a large bowl. Add the rest of the fruit and mix in the orange juice. Refrigerate the fruit and watermelon until a half hour before serving. Arrange the fruit in the melon. Sprinkle the mint on top.

A note on pineapple: They can be tricky little monsters that rarely reveal themselves without a struggle. They sound like Scorpios don't they? The best way to tell if a pineapple is ripe is to sniff the base. If it smells like a pineapple it is ripe but if it smells like fermented fruit, it is over ripe. Also, pull out one of the top leaves. If it pulls out easily the pineapple is ripe.

Asparagus Rolls

This is another recipe that you can use for a crowd. Asparagus, besides being majorly delicious, is also very good for the circulatory system. You might have to convince the more health-freaky Aquarian that pancetta isn't a bad thing. Just show them the brown bread. That will convince them to eat something as "evil" as pork.

20 fresh asparagus spears
¼ cup extra-virgin olive oil
2 teaspoons kosher salt
2 teaspoons freshly ground black pepper
3 garlic cloves, minced
1 lemon, juiced
20 slices pancetta

20 slices multi-grain bread, crusts removed
10 ounces of mascarpone cheese
2 tablespoons fresh chives, minced
1 tablespoon fresh tarragon, minced
¼ cup butter, melted
3 tablespoons Parmigiano-Reggiano cheese, grated

Serves 10

Preheat the oven to 500 degrees.

Wash the asparagus and snap off the tough ends (see note on page 137.) Place them in a single layer on a baking sheet. Pour the olive oil over the asparagus and roll them around so they are coated with a light film of oil. Sprinkle with salt, pepper and garlic. Roast in the oven for about 8–10 minutes until the thickest part can be speared with a fork. Don't let them get mushy. Remove from the oven and pour the lemon juice over them.

A note on bread: A lot of breads say "whole grain" but when you read the list of ingredients they say "wheat flour." Wheat flour is not a whole grain. It is just white flour with a bit less of the germ removed. For a whole grain flour be sure the ingredient list says "100 percent whole grain flour." I am partial to spelt and buckwheat flours

Reduce the oven temperature to 350 degrees.

In a medium sauté pan over medium heat, cook the pancetta until well browned but not burnt – about 8 minutes. Remove to a plate that has been covered with paper towels to drain.

If the bread is thick, flatten the slices a bit with a rolling pan.

In a medium mixing bowl, combine the mascarpone, chives and tarragon. Crumble the pancetta on top and mix well.

Spread a tablespoon of the cheese mix onto each slice of bread. Place a spear of asparagus on top and roll it up. Place the seam side down in a lightly greased baking sheet. Brush the top of the bread with the melted butter and sprinkle with the grated cheese.

Bake for about 15–20 minutes, until the cheese is lightly browned and bubbling. Serve warm.

Meat & Fish

Pollock with Berry Prosecco Sauce

Aquarians have a tremendous sense of brotherhood and shared responsibility. Serving sustainable fish is a sure way to their hearts. I had a similar recipe in Maine with salmon, which you can substitute here for the pollock. I just wanted to feature another sustainable fish because wild salmon gets the entire spotlight these days.

1 teaspoon extra-virgin olive oil
1 small bunch shallots, diced
1 teaspoon kosher salt
1 teaspoon freshly ground black pepper
3 cups blueberries, slightly crushed

Serves 4

½ bottle Prosecco
½ teaspoon red pepper flakes
¼ cup soy sauce
4 teaspoons freshly squeezed lemon juice
2 pounds pollock fillets
2 tablespoons fresh chives, diced

Preheat the oven to 400 degrees.

Make the sauce first. Heat the oil in a large saucepan over medium heat, add the shallots, salt and pepper and sauté until they begin to turn brown – about 2 minutes. Add the blueberries and Prosecco. Reduce the heat to low and allow the sauce to simmer until it reduces by a little less than half.

While the sauce is cooking, stir together the red pepper, soy sauce and lemon juice in a medium mixing bowl. Add the fish and coat well with mixture on all sides.

Grease a baking dish with olive oil spray. Place the fish in the dish in a single layer and bake for 20–30 minutes. The fish is done when it flakes with a fork.

Pour the warm Prosecco sauce over the fish, decorate with the chives and serve immediately.

A note on Prosecco: It is an Italian white wine that has a bit of bubble to it. It doesn't have the tiny bubbles of champagne and for me is much less sweet than true bubbly.

A note on fish: Do you like the idea of sustainable fish? That is very Aquarian of you. Visit this website for other sustainable fish sources www.sustainable-fish.com. I like a website that says it all in the title, don't you?

Wild Boar Ragú

Ah ha – you though I was going with the touchy-feely fish again! Get used to sudden changes when you deal with an Aquarian. Ruled by Uranus, the only planet to revolve on its side, Aquarius is all about quick stops and starts and thunderbolts when you least expect them.

Boar isn't in every grocery store freezer; – too bad, because I had it in Italy and it was delicious. Boar is also very low in fat. You can substitute its cousin pork if you must. (Tell the Aquarian it is boar if you want – they will believe you.)

The boar has to marinate overnight, so plan accordingly.

2 pounds wild boar shoulder, cut into one inch pieces
3 sprigs rosemary
3 tablespoons peppercorns
2 tablespoons kosher salt
1 bottle red wine
3 tablespoons extra-virgin olive oil
2 garlic cloves, diced

1 small carrot, finely chopped
1 small celery stalk, finely chopped
1 small onion, finely chopped
1 28-ounce can of crushed tomatoes
   (or see page 21 for my roasted tomatoes)
3 cups beef stock
2 cups red wine

Serves 6

Place the boar, rosemary, peppercorns, salt and wine in large bowl; cover and refrigerate overnight.

Preheat the oven to 375 degrees.

Remove the boar from the refrigerator, strain and discard the wine, rosemary and peppercorns. Heat the olive oil in a Dutch oven over medium heat. Add the garlic, carrot, celery and onion and sauté until the onion begins to get translucent – about 10 minutes. Add the meat and lightly brown on all sides – about 2–3 minutes per side. Pour in the tomatoes, stock and wine.

Place the pan in the oven and cook for 2 hours. After 1 hour check that there is still enough liquid in the pan. The meat should be just covered.

Serve immediately over rice or pasta.

Olive, Eggplant Caponata

Although Aquarius is an Air Sign it is symbolized by the water-bearer. I told you they could be confusing. Between the air and the water and their own quick moving minds. Aquarians are all about the flow of things. Sometimes when they are stuck their blood suffers. Olives are very high in Vitamin E which helps prevent blood clots and promotes good blood movement throughout the body. This caponata recipe is full of wonderful olives and is also easy for the Aquarian to eat while being glued to the computer or one of their many other electrical gadgets.

½ cup extra-virgin olive oil
6 garlic cloves, minced
2 medium white onions, diced
1 medium eggplant, diced
1 medium celery stalk, diced
1 medium green pepper, diced
1 teaspoon kosher salt

1 teaspoon freshly ground black pepper
3 teaspoons capers
½ cup tomato sauce
¼ teaspoon balsamic vinegar
2 teaspoons unsweeted chocolate, grated
1 cup pitted green olives
½ cup fresh basil leaves, gently minced

Serves 6 – 8

Heat the oil in a large sauté pan over medium heat. Add the garlic and sauté for about 2 minutes, until it just starts to brown. Remove to a medium bowl. Place the onions in the pan and sauté for about 8 minutes, until they are soft and browned. Add the eggplant, celery, green pepper, salt and pepper and sauté another 10 minutes. The eggplant and celery should be soft and lightly browned.

Add the capers, tomato sauce, vinegar and chocolate and stir well. Add the garlic back in with the green olives.

Continue to cook, stirring often until the eggplant and celery are soft and the liquids are all absorbed – about 20 minutes.

Remove from the heat and cool to room temperature. Sprinkle the basil leaves on top just before serving.

You can serve with crackers or baguette rounds.

To Their Health

Opposites Attract: Stretching your Aquarius South Node

Aquarius is on the axis with Leo. While Aquarius is learning the lesson of brotherhood and unity, Leo is all about self and how they reflect in the eyes of the world around them. Leo is the king, remember. Aquarius has to be surrounded by friends and has to be sure everyone has their exact fair share, so it might be hard to get them to be a little bit self-centered. However, if they are dealing with a South Node in Aquarius, being a bit selfish and decadent is just what the universe has ordered. Tell them that there are lots of lobsters out there – so much so that as I write this the price of lobster has never been lower because of a glut. So it really is sustainable and mac and cheese is "everyman" food. They won't know they are getting a taste of Leo elegance.

Lobster Mac and Cheese

1 teaspoon extra-virgin olive oil
3 tablespoons kosher salt, divided
1 ½ pounds elbow macaroni
1 quart milk
4 tablespoons butter, softened
6 tablespoons all-purpose flour
12 ounces Gruyere cheese, grated, divided

12 ounces Cheddar cheese, grated
12 ounces Fontina cheese, grated
2 teaspoons freshly ground black pepper
1 teaspoon freshly grated nutmeg
2 pounds lobster meat, shelled, cooked and diced

Serves 6

Preheat the oven to 350 degrees.

In a large soup pot, bring 4 quarts of water, 2 tablespoons of the salt and oil to a boil over high heat. Add the macaroni and cook about 6–8 minutes, until they are still firm.

While the macaroni is cooking, heat the milk in a large saucepan over medium-low heat. Don't let it boil over. Add the butter and then whisk in the flour until it is well incorporated. Remove from the heat and whisk in the cheeses, saving 2 ounces of the Gruyere for the topping, the nutmeg, the remaining salt and pepper. When the cheeses are melted (you may have to put over very low heat if the melting process stops) stir in the lobster and mix well.

Drain the macaroni and stir a bit of the cheese mixture in to temper it. Add a bit more cheese mixture and stir well; then toss the macaroni in with the rest of the cheese mixture. Keep stirring until everything is well combined.

Pour into a well-greased 4-quart casserole and bake 30–40 minutes until it is bubbling. Sprinkle the remaining Gruyere over top and serve immediately.

Dessert

Floating Island

Aquarians can be mesmerized by this pretty dessert which is separate little beautiful islands all coming together as one and then separating and then coming back together. It is the perfect symbol of Aquarians' need for balance and freedom and brotherhood.

1 quart milk, divided
1 cup sugar, divided
1 vanilla bean, split lengthways in half
8 large eggs, separated
¼ teaspoon freshly grated nutmeg

Serves 8

For caramel sauce:
    4 tablespoons unsalted butter
    1 cup brown sugar
    1 tablespoon vanilla extract
Bring to a boil in a medium saucepan. Reduce the heat and simmer for 10 minutes.

In a medium saucepan over medium heat, warm ½ of the milk, ½ cup of the sugar and the scrapings from the vanilla bean. Stir gently until the sugar dissolves. When the mixture begins to boil, reduce the heat to low.

In a large mixing bowl, beat the egg whites at medium speed until they form soft peaks. Add 1 tablespoon of the sugar and continue to beat until the peaks are stiff. Take a large unslotted serving spoon and scoop up 8 spoonfuls of the egg mixture and gently place them in the milk. Don't crowd the pot and do these one at the time. Poaching time is about 2–3 minutes on each side. Remove them to serving dishes.

While the meringues are poaching, whisk together the rest of sugar, nutmeg and the egg yolks in a large mixing bowl. Pour into a medium sauce pan with the rest of the milk and cook over low heat until the sugar is dissolved and you can coat the back of a spoon with the mixture – about 4 minutes. Gently pour this around the poached islands, being careful not to smash them.

Chill in the refrigerator for about 1 hour.

Drizzle cooled caramel sauce over the islands just before serving.

A note on nutmeg: Buy the actual nutmeg and grate it as needed. It is much better than the pre-grated stuff that sits on the store shelf for a couple of centuries.... or so it seems!

Famous People
with
Aquarius South Node –
Leo North Node

Mahatma Gandhi –

He used hunger strikes to protest the caste system and other human inequities. While the spotlight was on him (Leo Sun), he used the best aspects of his Aquarian South Node and its innate belief that all men are brothers and should be treated as equals.

Greta Garbo –

The enigmatic star was allegedly a follower of a nutritionist of the 1930s named Gayelord Hauser. He was known for such "yummy" morsels as hamburgers made of wild rice and chopped hazelnuts, mixed with an egg. All of this was fried in soybean oil. Remember, I said Aquarians have a pronounced quirky streak.

Albert Einstein showed his Aquarius North Node card with his food choices. Ahead of the curve, he was a vegetarian well before it was popular, and claimed his favorite foods were oatmeal and pancakes. See what I mean about Aquarians being ah… unique?

pisces

Chapter 14

Pisces is symbolized by two fish swimming in opposite directions. It is the other sign of duality in addition to Gemini. Pisces is often lost here on Earth. It vibrates to the 12th house, the house that is our connection to the universe, to god, to the immortal. It is the most spiritual of signs and Pisceans are much happier floating in the universal eithers than in the day-to-day drudgery of Earth. There is an escapist element to Pisces because they have the memory of what it is like to be beyond the physical – in the peaceful seas of the heavens.

Ruled by Neptune, the planet named for the god of the expansive seas. I often think of Pisces as a graceful whale in the ocean. It is so huge but cuts through the water with elegance and ease. However, when taken out of its watery element the beautiful whale flails around and eventually dies. Pisces is always looking to go back to the sea or beyond the sky.

Positive aspects of Pisces include:
a deep sympathetic nature, spirituality, creativity and artistic ability.

Shadow aspects of Pisces include:
escapism via drinking, drugs or gambling, lack of direction and focus, "Christ complex"
– sense of martyrdom and the ability to suffer for the sake of suffering.

Foodie aspects of Pisces include:
foods from the sea, calming foods, and food with a bit of whimsy.

Famous People with Pisces Rising

Whitney Houston – Whitney had the escapist tendencies of Pisces and other issues that made it difficult for her to break away from Neptune's hold. Her eating disorders were also part of Pisces need not only to escape but also to make themselves suffer.

Alfred Hitchcock – His ability to create worlds through his movies that appeal to those born long after his death is a truly Piscean attribute. I think it is hysterical that he had a penchant for blue food and at least once served his guests food laced with blue food coloring including the fish and soup. Well, blue is the color of the sea and sky, after all.

Scallop Bruschetta

Although the great ocean that Pisces the fish swims in is the cosmic ocean, they are the wateriest of the water signs. We need to bring the fish back to the water from time to time so they can reorient themselves. Pisces is the other sign of duality (along with Gemini) and they need to find the calm of the water when life is a bit overwhelming, which it often is for them. If you look at the glyph for Pisces the two fish are swimming in different directions, poor dears.

 I had this dish in, where else, Maine and have tried to recreate it here.

Appetizer

2 tablespoons extra-virgin olive oil, divided
1 cup cherry tomatoes, diced
1 cup canned artichoke hearts, diced
2 tablespoons white onions, minced
5 capers
4 tablespoons grated Parmigiano-Reggiano cheese

Serves 6

2 teaspoons lemon juice
1 teaspoon kosher salt
1 teaspoon fresh thyme, minced
6 scallops, cleaned
1–2 garlic cloves, minced
12 crostini rounds – about 1 ½ inches around

In a medium sauté pan over medium heat, heat 1 tablespoon of the oil and then add the tomatoes, artichokes and onions. Cook, stirring often, until the artichokes begin to brown – about 2–3 minutes. Remove from the heat to a medium bowl and add the capers, cheese, lemon juice, salt and thyme.

Add the scallops to the pan (if it is very dry add a little more olive oil until it just coats the bottom of the pan) and sauté on each side about 4 minutes, until they are lightly browned.

While the scallops are cooking, brush the remaining olive oil on the crostini. Rub the garlic cloves on the crostini and discard the garlic.

On each crostini place a layer of the tomato mixture and ½ of a scallop. Serve immediately.

A note on crostini: You can make crostini out of any hard bread, even multigrain baguettes. Just cut them into one inch slices, brush with some extra-virgin olive oil and stick under a low broiler for a few minutes or put on a grill. When it is cool, it is crostini.

Soup

Jean Garofalo Porte's
Tomato Soup with Ditali Pasta

Pisces needs calm – they often have neuroses and other issues that set their nerves on edge.

My mother made a very comforting tomato soup – and even though I didn't like other tomato soups in my youth, I liked this one. Well, she was a Pisces Sun after all!

4 tablespoons extra-virgin olive oil
2 medium white onions, diced
2 medium celery stalks, diced
2 medium carrots, diced
5–6 garlic cloves, minced
3 tablespoons fresh thyme, minced
3 tablespoons fresh oregano, minced
3 tablespoons fresh flat-leaf Italian parsley, minced
2 teaspoons kosher salt
1 teaspoon freshly ground black pepper

Serves 6

16 ounces chicken stock (see page 44)
3 28-ounce cans for whole peeled tomatoes
   (or see page 21 for roasted tomatoes)
½ pound ditali pasta or any small pasta
   like elbow macaroni
¼ cup fresh basil leaves
¼ cup Parmigiano-Reggiano cheese,
   freshly grated

Heat the oil in a large soup pot over medium heat. Add the onions, celery and carrots and sauté about 5 minutes until the onions start to become translucent. Add the garlic and sauté another 2 minutes until the garlic starts to brow but not burn. Stir in the thyme, oregano, parsley, salt and pepper.

Stir in the chicken stock (you can do vegetable stock to make this dish vegetarian) and the tomatoes. Reduce the heat and simmer for about an hour, stirring often. Remove from the heat and allow to cool before you spoon into the food processor. Be careful with hot soup. Pulse the soup a few times until it is smooth. You can also use an immersion blender.

Just before serving, return to the stove to medium-high heat and stir in the ditali. Cook, stirring often, for about 6 minutes until it is *al dente*. Add the basil, sprinkle the cheese over top and serve immediately.

Seafood Lasagna

This pasta has two advantages – it reminds the Pisces of the sea and provides the comfort that they so often need. It is so hard for Pisces to leave the spiritual realm and live here on Earth so they need all the comfort they can get!

See my note on page 191 about cheese and fish.

3 cups Italian tomato sauce or "gravy"
  (see page 24)
3 tablespoons kosher salt
3 tablespoons extra-virgin olive oil, divided
1 ½ pounds lasagna noodles
1 cup mushrooms, sliced thinly
½ pound medium shrimp
½ pound scallops, cut in half

Serves 8

½ pound crab meat, cut into small pieces
¼ cup white wine
1 teaspoon freshly ground black pepper
3 tablespoons fresh flat-leaf Italian parsley, minced
1 pound ricotta cheese
8 ounces mozzarella cheese, sliced thinly
1 cup basil leaves

Pasta

Make the gravy first and keep it warm over low heat.

In a large soup pot bring the 3 quarts of water, salt and 1 tablespoon of the oil to a boil over medium heat. Add the lasagna noodles and cook about 8–10 minutes until they are *al dente*.

In the meantime, heat the other 2 tablespoons of oil in a medium sauté pan over medium heat, add the mushrooms and cook 5–7 minutes until they are lightly browned. Add the shrimp, scallops, crab, wine and pepper and cook another 5 minutes.

When the lasagna noodles are done, drain them in the sink, transfer to a large bowl and ladle about 2 or 3 spoonfuls of gravy over the noodles and gently stir to keep them from sticking together.

In a medium mixing bowl combine the parsley and ricotta cheese. Spray the bottom and sides of a 3-quart baking dish with olive oil cooking spray. Ladle a thin layer of gravy on the bottom of the dish. Then make alternating layers of lasagna noodles, seafood mixture, ricotta cheese and gravy until the dish is full. The last layer should be the gravy.

Top with a layer of mozzarella cheese and decorate with basil leaves.

Bake for 30–40 minutes until the cheese is melted and browned and lasagna is bubbling. Rest for about 20–30 minutes before cutting. Serve with hot gravy on the side.

A note on no-cook lasagna noodles: Really? Even a fast-moving Gemini can take a few extra minutes to cook with "real" noodles. Come on now. We don't need to eat cardboard.

Veggies & Fruit

Quinoa with Roasted Root Veggies

In addition to having some say over our nervous system, Pisces also controls the immune system. Auto immune illness, allergies, etc. are all traced to Neptune and Pisces. Our diet can help a great deal when it comes to controlling auto immune flare-ups. Eating lots of veggies and good grains is important to keeping auto-immunity under control.

Remember to look at the 6th house for real insight into someone's health. Even a sturdy looking Aries can have a weak constitution if Pisces is hovering around their 6th.

¼ cup extra-virgin olive oil	3 teaspoons kosher salt, divided
3 pounds butternut squash	1 tablespoon freshly ground black pepper
3 pounds sweet potatoes	4 tablespoons balsamic vinegar
3 pounds fresh medium beets, (remove tops and greens)	2 cups quinoa
2 large parsnips	2 quarts chicken (or veggie) stock (see page 44)
4 large carrots, scraped and diced	1 cup white wine
2 heads garlic, peeled and quartered	

Serves 8 – 10

Again, I never understand why people kill themselves removing the skin from things like butternut squash when it is raw. Roast them first and when they are cool the skins come off with ease! Aries, you don't have to prove your strength and Capricorn, it is okay to take the easy way sometimes. Let it go.

Preheat the oven to 450 degrees.

Put the oil in a large roasting pan. Add the squash, potatoes, beets and parsnips in the pan and cook until they are soft.

The beets and parsnips should be done in 35–45 minutes, the potatoes in about an hour and the squash about an hour and thirty minutes. Test them with a fork every 10 minutes so they don't overcook.

When the veggies are cool to the touch, remove the skin from the squash and the parsnips and the thick skin of the beets. Cut all of them into 1 inch cubes. Return them to the roasting pan, add the carrots and garlic. Sprinkle with half of the salt, and the pepper and vinegar and gently stir to coat all of the veggies.

Return to the oven and cook another 30 minutes until the carrots are tender.

In the meantime, place the quinoa in a medium sauce pan and sprinkle with the remaining salt. Add stock and wine and bring to a boil and then reduce the heat to medium. Cook 30–40 minutes until the quinoa is tender.

Place the quinoa in a large serving platter and spoon the veggies on top. Serve immediately.

A note on vinegar: What is the deal with balsamic vinegar? We didn't hear of it here in the States until about 15 years ago when, according to legend, Luciano Pavarotti began to talk about the great vinegar from his home town of Modena, Italy which was made from Trebbiano grapes in aged barrels. There was a time, in those early years, when people were putting it on everything and frankly it got a bit dumb. However, in this dish it is great.

♈ ♉ ♊ ♋ ♌ ♍ ♎ ♏ ♐ ♑ ♒ ♓

Kale with Ginger and Scallions

The best kale I have ever eaten is from an adorable tea house in Washington, D.C. called Ching Ching Cha's. I know it has ginger, soy and scallions and this comes close to theirs, although I have to admit, theirs is always better than mine. This is a great anti-inflammatory dish.

1 ½ pounds kale, stems removed
3 tablespoons sesame oil
3 garlic cloves, minced
3 large scallions, diced
4 teaspoons fresh ginger, minced
4 tablespoons light soy sauce

Serves 8

Tear the kale into bite-sized portions and wash thoroughly. In a medium skillet, heat the sesame oil over low heat. Add the garlic and scallions and cook 2–3 minutes until they start to brown. Add the ginger and then stir in the kale.

Cook the kale about 2 minutes until it begins to soften. Pour in the soy sauce, cover and cook another 3 minutes. The kale should be softened but still crunchy.

Serve immediately.

Meat & Fish

Mussels Marinara

My mother was a Pisces (March 7) and one of her favorite seafood dishes was Mussels Marinara. So this is for you, Mom.

3 tablespoons extra-virgin olive oil
2 small white onions, diced
4 garlic cloves, diced
1 cup red wine
3 14-ounce cans plum tomatoes
  (or see my roasted tomatoes on page 21)

2 tablespoons fresh oregano leaves, chopped
2 tablespoons fresh thyme, chopped
2 tablespoons fresh flat-leaf Italian parsley, chopped
4 pound mussels, cleaned and debearded

Serves 8

Clean* the mussels well under running water and discard any that are opened.

Heat the oil in a large sauté pan over medium heat. Add the onions and cook about 6 minutes until they start to get translucent. Add the garlic and cook another 2 minutes. Stir in the wine; lower the heat and cook, stirring occasionally, until the wine is reduced by about half. Add the tomatoes, spices and mussels and cook 10–15 minutes until the mussels open. Discard any that do not open.

Place the mussels in a large bowl and spoon the marinara sauce over top. Serve immediately.

*A note on cleaning mussels: It is best done by placing them in a large bowl filled with about 3 cups of water and a half cup of flour for about 45 minutes. This helps disgorge any sand inside. Then drain and rinse the mussels. If they still look dirty scrub them with a small brush under running water. Then to debeard the mussels pinch the beard – or the furry part – between your thumb and first finger, then using a side-to-side motion, firmly yank that sucker out.

Tilapia with Feta

I first saw a similar recipe with shrimp and lemon. However, I have a lot of friends who are allergic to shrimp and I wasn't too crazy about the lemon and tomato sauce together. I changed it for a non-allergenic fish and zapped the lemons.

Fennel is also full of antioxidants and helps to boost the immune system. Pisces needs a boost when life gets too hard, which for them can happen weekly.

2 tablespoons extra-virgin olive oil
1 ½ cups fennel bulb, diced
4 garlic cloves, minced
¼ cup white wine
1 14-ounce can diced tomatoes
   (or use my roasted tomatoes on page 21)
1 teaspoon fresh oregano, diced

1 teaspoon fresh thyme, diced
½ teaspoon red pepper flakes
5 ounces feta cheese, crumbled
3 tablespoons fresh flat-leaf Italian parsley, minced
3 teaspoons kosher salt
3 teaspoons freshly ground black pepper
8 4-ounce filets tilapia

Serves 8

Preheat the oven to 400 degrees.

Heat the olive oil in a large heavy ovenproof skillet over low heat. Add the fennel and sauté for 8–10 minutes, until tender. Add the garlic and cook for 1 minute. Raise the heat and add the wine, tomatoes, oregano, thyme and red pepper flakes. After it comes to a boil, reduce the heat to medium and cook, stirring often for 15 minutes.

While that is cooking, combine the feta and parsley in a small bowl. Set aside.

Salt and pepper both sides of the fish. Lay the fish into the skillet on top of the tomato mixture and bake for 10 minutes. Remove from the oven.

Sprinkle the feta and parsley over the fish. Place the skillet back in the oven and bake for another 10–15 minutes.

Serve immediately.

To Their Health

A note on cutlets: *What is a chicken cutlet? In some places you can actually purchase pre-cut chicken cutlets. If you can't find them get some skinless, boneless chicken breasts, slice them in half and then press down on them gently. They will mimic the size of a cutlet.*

Chicken or Veal with Onions and Eggs

My Mom used to make this with veal but those were the days before it was politically incorrect. Chicken or veal both work fine and will pack a punch of protein to calm the Pisces nerves. They can also use the home-cooking appeal of this dish that will remind me them of Mom and the good old days before life got too hard for them. For Pisces that would be around the age of eight.

½ cup extra-virgin olive oil
2 large white onions, sliced thinly
½ teaspoon sugar
1 teaspoon kosher salt
1 teaspoon freshly ground black pepper
6 pieces veal scaloppini or chicken cutlets
2 teaspoons fresh thyme, minced

1 teaspoon fresh oregano, minced
1 cup chicken stock (see page 44)
3 tablespoons all-purpose flour
1 cup white wine
6 large eggs
2 tablespoons fresh flat-leaf Italian parsley, minced

Serves 6

Heat an electric frying pan to 250 degrees. Add the oil and when warm add the onions, sugar, salt and pepper. Slowly caramelize the onions, stirring frequently, until the onions are lightly browned – about 20–30 minutes.

Raise the heat to 350 degrees.

Add the meat and brown about 3 minutes on each side; add the thyme and oregano.

In a medium bowl, mix the chicken stock and flour until there are no clumps. Slowly pour into the frying pan, stirring constantly. Stir in the wine. Cook another 15 minutes until the liquid is reduced by half.

Just before serving, gently crack the eggs over the chicken. Cover and cook until the egg whites become opaque. Sprinkle the meat with parsley and serve immediately with the juice spooned over the meat.

Opposites Attract: Stretching Your Pisces South Node

Pisces need to learn to get their feet on the ground. Their axis opposites are very earthy – very practical Virgos. What better way to feel more earthy than to eat some beef? I have added lots of veggies and healthy ginger because you know how the Virgo is about being healthy. For that reason, get organic beef too!

Wok cooking is done over high heat. It will appeal to the Fire Signs but please be careful. Hot oil on the skin is no fun and will leave one nasty scar.

Ginger Beef Stir Fry

2 ¾ cups freshly squeezed orange juice
4 teaspoons fresh ginger, diced
2 garlic cloves, diced
1 teaspoon chili powder
3 tablespoons soy sauce
2 pounds boneless beef sirloin steak,
    cut into thin strips
1 tablespoon extra-virgin olive oil
2 cups broccoli florets, diced
2 cups red and yellow peppers, diced
1 medium white onion, diced
1 cup carrots, sliced thinly
1 cup button mushrooms, sliced
1 teaspoon kosher salt
2 teaspoons freshly ground black pepper
½ cup fresh basil leaves

Serves 8 – 10

In a large mixing bowl combine the orange juice, ginger, garlic, chili powder, soy sauce and steak. Mix well. Cover and refrigerate for 2 hours, turning once.

In a wok or large sauté pan heat the olive oil over high heat. Add the broccoli, peppers, onion, carrots, mushrooms, salt and pepper and cook until the peppers are soft and the onion begin to get translucent – about 6–8 minutes. Strain the beef mixture of all but 2 tablespoons of orange juice. Stir the beef and the 2 tablespoons of orange juice into the pan and cook, stirring often, another 4 minutes. Add the basil leaves, and serve immediately. You can serve over noodles or a bed of brown rice.

Dessert

Jean Garofalo Porte's Easter Ricotta Pie

Pisces are often called the martyrs of the Zodiac. They often place themselves in positions of service to others and often pay off a load of karma in their Piscean lifetimes. For dessert, I am offering them an Italian cheese cake that my mother made at Easter – the time Christians celebrate the martyrdom of Jesus.

Make the pie crust on page 207. It will cover the bottom of the dish. I prefer to cut the carbs and do it crustless but either works.

3 pounds ricotta cheese
10 eggs
1 ½ cups confectioners sugar
1 can evaporated milk
1 teaspoon fresh orange juice

1 teaspoon fresh lemon juice
Rind of 1 medium orange, minced
1 ½ teaspoons ground cinnamon
½ teaspoon freshly grated nutmeg
1 cup mandarin oranges*

Fills one 9 by 14 inch baking dish.

Preheat the oven to 400 degrees.

If you are not using a crust, generously spray the bottom and sides of the baking dish.

Mix together all of the ingredients in a large bowl. Be sure there are no lumps. Pour into the dish and bake for 15 minutes. Reduce the heat to 325 degrees and cook another 60–70 minutes until the cheese is set and the top just begins to brown. Wow, this is fast enough for even a Gemini to love.

Cool on a cake rack and then refrigerate until ready to serve.

*Mom used maraschino cherries but those were the days before the red dye scare. We were only afraid of Red Russia in those days.

A note on confectioners sugar: It is really sugar that is cut very fine and is mixed with a little bit of anti-caking material like cornstarch. There are actually various grades of fineness of confectioners sugar that I guess are of great concern to great bakers. The sugar you purchase in your local grocery will do for this recipe.

Famous People with
Pisces South Node –
Virgo North Node

Wolfgang Amadeus Mozart –

Anyone who can hear music in his head and write it down with no edits has to have a ton of Pisces in his chart! He was connecting with the universe! Of course, he had some of the shadow aspects as well and had a hard time grounding himself on Earth as Virgo asks. Then again it is said that his favorite dish was liver dumplings and sauerkraut. You can't get more earthy than that!

Bono –

The musician certainly has Piscean compassion as exhibited by his extensive charitable work. By the way, he claims the reason why he wears sunglasses all the time is eye sensitivity although he admits it is also part a privacy issue. No kidding, Bono! You have your Moon and Neptune (the ruler of your South Node) in Scorpio – that sign of secrecy! Back to Pisces, the massive humanitarian efforts for which he has been nominated for the Nobel Peace Prize are a true nod to using the most positive elements of his South Node. The work he does is to provide food and care to the poor, which is a Virgo issue. This is a perfect example of someone who uses their South Node in service to the North. It is reported that his favorite food is fish and chips and his favorite drink is Jack Daniels. Yup, that is still Pisces talking!

Elizabeth Taylor was so very Piscean. Not only was she a Pisces Sun, she also had a Pisces North Node. Who else could have those dream-like Piscean eyes but Ms. Taylor? Her battles with food and other addictions were also sadly Piscean as well. It is said that she craved the chili at Chasen's restaurant so much that she even had it flown to Rome when she was filming "Cleopatra."

index

aries

taurus

gemini

♈ ♉ ♊ ♋ ♌ ♍ ♎ ♏ ♐ ♑ ♒ ♓

cancer

♈ ♉ ♊ ♋ ♌ ♍ ♎ ♏ ♐ ♑ ♒ ♓

leo

virgo

libra

♈ ♉ ♊ ♋ ♌ ♍ ♎ ♏ ♐ ♑ ♒ ♓

scorpio

sagittarius

♈ ♉ ♊ ♋ ♌ ♍ ♎ ♏ ♐ ♑ ♒ ♓

capricorn

♈ ♉ ♊ ♋ ♌ ♍ ♎ ♏ ♐ ♑ ♒ ♓

aquarius

♈ ♉ ♊ ♋ ♌ ♍ ♎ ♏ ♐ ♑ ♒ ♓

pisces

about the author:

Me and Mom in the kitchen circa 1961.

Joan started "playing" with Astrology when she was in grammar school. She always had a fixation with the planets – Pluto being her favorite (surprise she is Scorpio Sun!) Yes, Pluto is still a planet to her! She put her astrology "toys" away when she grew up and went into the "real world," sadly convinced that it was time to do more important things. The universe and her North Node in Sagittarius woke her up in her mid-thirties after which she began an intensive study of Western astrology.

According to Joan, "Modern Man takes for granted the Sun and how its energy propels and sustains life. Moon energy controls the tides yet we ignore the other more personal influences it has on our bodies and lives. We have lost the art of appreciating and reading the stars as messengers from the god and goddess. Humanity has disconnected from its source and consequently suffers emotionally, spiritually and physically."

"Each person is born with a map – a soul map – that is his or her astrological chart. It is a map through the maze of life that shows the karma we need to balance our soul's desire for a life that leads to enhanced soul growth. I simply read the map – illustrating where you have been and where you are going to make your journey through life less bumpy."

With this cook book Joan is combining her astrological knowledge with her lifelong love of cooking in her own inimitable way.

She is the author of http://www.joansastrology.blogspot.com

Her other book is *Fortyish: Lessons For the Ages From a Baby Boomer.*

CPSIA information can be obtained at www.ICGtesting.com
Printed in the USA
LVOW02s1443021013

355107LV00001B/1/P